WORSHIP

**THE REASON WE WERE CREATED—
COLLECTED INSIGHTS FROM**

A. W. TOZER

MOODY PUBLISHERS
CHICAGO

Edited by Kevin P. Emmert
Interior and Cover Design: Erik M. Peterson
Cover art by Unhidden Media, unhiddenmedia.com

Library of Congress Cataloging-in-Publication Data

Names: Tozer, A. W. (Aiden Wilson), 1897-1963, author.
Title: Worship : the reason we were created--collected insights from A. W. Tozer / A. W. Tozer.
Description: Chicago : Moody Publishers, 2017. | Includes bibliographical references.
Identifiers: LCCN 2017025070 (print) | LCCN 2017028820 (ebook) | ISBN 9780802496126 | ISBN 9780802416032
Subjects: LCSH: Worship.
Classification: LCC BV10.3 (ebook) | LCC BV10.3 .T695 2017 (print) | DDC 248.3--dc23
LC record available at https://lccn.loc.gov/2017025070

ISBN: 978-0-8024-1603-2

We hope you enjoy this book from Moody Publishers. Our goal is to provide high-quality, thought-provoking books and products that connect truth to your real needs and challenges. For more information on other books and products written and produced from a biblical perspective, go to www.moodypublishers.com or write to:

Moody Publishers
820 N. LaSalle Boulevard
Chicago, IL 60610

1 3 5 7 9 10 8 6 4 2

Printed in the United States of America

CONTENTS

PUBLISHER'S NOTE

A. W. Tozer was a man who encountered the living God and made it his highest goal in life to worship Him in spirit and truth. Besides God, worship is perhaps the most important theme in Tozer's writings, and the eleven selections that follow are a small sampling of his teachings on the topic.

Tozer's main goal as a pastor and writer was to help people love and worship the God who created them. With prophetic vigor, he urges us to recognize God's call to us so that we might live life as He intended in His presence and for His glory. What you will encounter in the following pages is a call to recognize that worship is the chief reason we were created and that the object of our worship—the triune God—is far greater than we could ever imagine. As Tozer himself said,

Yes, worship of the loving God is man's whole reason for existence. That is why we are born, and that is why we are born again from above. That is why we were created, and that is why we have been recreated. That is why there was a genesis at the beginning, and that is why there is a re-genesis, called regeneration.

That is also why there is a church. The Christian church exists to worship God first of all. Everything else must come second or third or fourth or fifth. (*Whatever Happened to Worship*, p. 50)

While these are the words of one man who died decades ago, they testify to the timeless truth that everything in this life and all our ambitions pale in comparison to knowing and magnifying the one true God who is the Lord of all. Tozer would want you not to focus on him or his writing, but on the ever-loving and almighty God. May each selection in this volume point you to Him and inspire you to worship Him in awe and gratitude.

WHAT HAPPENED TO OUR WORSHIP?

I know your deeds, that you are neither cold nor hot.
I wish you were either one or the other! So, because
you are lukewarm—neither hot nor cold—I am
about to spit you out of my mouth.

REVELATION 3:15–16

C hristian churches have come to the dangerous time pre-
dicted long ago. It is a time when we can pat one another on the back, congratulate ourselves, and join in the glad
refrain, "We are rich, and increased with goods, and have need
of nothing!"

It certainly is true that hardly anything is missing from our
churches these days—except the most important thing. We are
missing the genuine and sacred offering of ourselves and our
worship to the God and Father of our Lord Jesus Christ.

In the message of the Revelation, the angel of the church of
the Laodiceans made this charge and this appeal (3:17, 19):

"Thou sayest, I am rich, and increased with goods, and have need of nothing. . . . As many as I love, I rebuke and chasten: be zealous therefore, and repent."

My own loyalties and responsibilities are and always will be with the strongly evangelical, Bible-believing, Christ-honoring churches. We have been surging forward. We are building great churches and large congregations. We are boasting about high standards and we are talking a lot about revival. But I have a question, and it is not just rhetoric: "What has happened to our worship?"

The reply of many is, "We are rich and have need of nothing. Doesn't that say something about God's blessing?" Did you know that the often-quoted Jean-Paul Sartre describes his turning to philosophy and hopelessness as a turning away from a secularistic church? He says, "I did not recognize in the fashionable God who was taught me, Him who was waiting for my soul. I needed a Creator; I was given a big businessman!"

None of us is as concerned as we should be about the image we really project to the community around us. At least not when we profess to belong to Jesus Christ and still fail to show forth His love and compassion as we should. We who are the fundamentalists and the "orthodox" Christians have gained the reputation of being "tigers"—great fighters for the truth. Our hands are heavy with callouses from the brass knuckles we have worn as we beat on the liberals. Because of the meaning of our Christian faith for a lost world, we are obligated to stand up for the truth and to contend for the faith when necessary.

But there is a better way, even in our dealing with those who are liberals in faith and theology. We can do a whole lot more for them by being Christlike than we can by figuratively beating them over the head with our knuckles. The liberals tell us they cannot believe the Bible. They tell us they cannot believe that Jesus Christ was the unique Son of God. At least most of them are honest about it. Moreover, I am certain we are not going to make them bow the knee by cursing them. If we are led by the Spirit of God and if we show forth the love of God this world needs, we become the "winsome saints."

The strange and wonderful thing about it is that truly winsome and loving saints do not even know about their attractiveness. The great saints of past eras did not know they were great saints. If someone had told them, they would not have believed it, but those around them knew that Jesus was living His life in them.

I think we join the winsome saints when God's purposes in Christ become clear to us. We join them when we begin to worship God because He is who He is.

Sometimes evangelical Christians seem to be fuzzy and uncertain about the nature of God and His purposes in creation and redemption. In such instances, the preachers often are to blame. There are still preachers and teachers who say that Christ died so we would not drink and not smoke and not go to the theater.

No wonder people are confused! No wonder they fall into the habit of backsliding when such things are held up as the reason for salvation.

Jesus was born of a virgin, suffered under Pontius Pilate, died on the cross and rose from the grave to make worshipers out of rebels! He has done it all through grace. We are the recipients.

That may not sound dramatic, but it is God's revelation and God's way.

Another example of our wrong thinking about God is the attitude of so many that God is now a charity case. He is a kind of frustrated foreman who cannot find enough help. He stands at the wayside asking how many will come to His rescue and begin to do His work.

Oh, if we would only remember who He is! God has never actually needed any of us—not one. But we pretend that He does and we make it a big thing when someone agrees "to work for the Lord."

We all should be willing to work for the Lord, but it is a matter of grace on God's part. I am of the opinion that we should not be concerned about working for God until we have learned the meaning and the delight of worshiping Him.

A worshiper can work with eternal quality in his work. But a worker who does not worship is only piling up wood, hay, and stubble for the time when God sets the world on fire.

I fear that there are many professing Christians who do not want to hear such statements about their "busy schedule," but it is the truth. God is trying to call us back to that for which He created us—to worship Him and to enjoy Him forever!

It is then, out of our deep worship, that we do His work.

I heard a college president say that the church is "suffering from a rash of amateurism." Any untrained, unprepared, unspiritual empty rattletrap of a person can start something religious and find plenty of followers who will listen and pay and promote it. It may become very evident that he or she had never heard from God in the first place.

These things are happening all around us because we are not worshipers. If we are truly among the worshipers we will not be spending our time with carnal or worldly religious projects.

All of the examples that we have in the Bible illustrate that glad and devoted and reverent worship is the normal employment of moral beings. Every glimpse that is given us of heaven and of God's created beings is always a glimpse of worship and rejoicing and praise, because God is who He is. The apostle John, in Revelation 4:10–11, gives us a plain portrayal of created beings around the throne of God. John speaks of the occupation of the elders in this way:

> The four and twenty elders fall down before him that sat on the throne, and worship him that liveth for ever and ever, and cast their crowns before the throne, saying, "Thou art worthy, O Lord, to receive glory and honour and power: for thou hast created all things, and for thy pleasure they are and were created."

I can safely say, on the authority of all that is revealed in the Word of God, that any man or woman on this earth who is bored and turned off by worship is not ready for heaven. But I can almost hear someone saying, "Is Tozer getting away from justification by faith? Haven't we always heard that we are justified and saved and on our way to heaven by faith?" I assure you that Martin Luther never believed in justification by faith more strongly than I do. I believe in justification by faith. I believe we are saved by having faith in the Son of God as Lord and Savior. But nowadays there is a deadly, automatic quality about getting saved. It bothers me greatly.

I say an "automatic" quality: "Put a nickel's worth of faith in

the slot, pull down the lever and take out the little card of salvation. Tuck it in your wallet and off you go!" After that, the man
or woman can say, "Yes, I'm saved." How does he or she know?
"I put the nickel in. I accepted Jesus and I signed the card." Very
good. There is nothing intrinsically wrong with signing a card.
It can be a helpful thing so we know who has made inquiry. But
really, my brother or sister, we are brought to God and to faith
and to salvation that we might worship and adore Him. We do
not come to God that we might be automatic Christians, cookie-
cutter Christians, Christians stamped out with a die.

God has provided His salvation that we might be, individually
and personally, vibrant children of God, loving God with all our
hearts and worshiping Him in the beauty of holiness.

This does not mean, and I am not saying, that we must all
worship alike. The Holy Spirit does not operate by anyone's
preconceived idea or formula. But this I know: when the Holy
Spirit of God comes among us with His anointing, we become
a worshiping people. This may be hard for some to admit, but
when we are truly worshiping and adoring the God of all grace
and of all love and of all mercy and of all truth, we may not be
quiet enough to please everyone.

I recall Luke's description of the throngs on that first
Palm Sunday:

The whole multitude of the disciples began to rejoice and
praise God with a loud voice for all the mighty works that
they had seen; saying, Blessed be the King that cometh
in the name of the Lord: peace in heaven, and glory in

the highest. And some of the Pharisees from among the multitude said unto him, Master, rebuke thy disciples. And he answered and said unto them, I tell you that, if these should hold their peace, the stones would immediately cry out. (19:37-40)

Let me say two things here. First, I do not believe it is necessarily true that we are worshiping God when we are making a lot of racket. But not infrequently worship is audible. When Jesus came into Jerusalem presenting Himself as Messiah there was a great multitude and there was a great noise. Doubtless many who joined in the singing and the praise had never been able to sing in the right key. When you have a group of people singing anywhere, you know that some of them will not be in tune. But this is the point to their worship: they were united in praises to God.

Second, I would warn those who are cultured, quiet, self-possessed, poised and sophisticated, that if they are embarrassed in church when some happy Christian says "Amen!" they may actually be in need of some spiritual enlightenment. The worshiping saints of God in the body of Christ have often been a little bit noisy. I hope you have read some of the devotionals left us by that dear old English saint, Lady Julian, who lived more than 600 years ago.

She wrote that one day she had been thinking about how high and lofty Jesus was, and yet how He Himself meets the humblest part of our human desire. She received such blessing within her being that she could not control herself. She let go with a shout and praised God out loud in Latin.

Translated into English, it would have come out "Well, glory to God!"

Now, if that bothers you, friend, it may be because you do not know the kind of spiritual blessings and delight the Holy Spirit is waiting to provide among God's worshiping saints.

Did you notice what Luke said about the Pharisees and their request that Jesus should rebuke His disciples for praising God with loud voices? Their ritual rules probably allowed them to whisper the words "Glory to God!", but it really pained them to hear anyone saying them out loud.

Jesus told the Pharisees in effect: "They are doing the right thing. God My Father and I and the Holy Ghost are to be worshiped. If men and women will not worship Me, the very rocks will shout My praises!"

Those religious Pharisees, polished and smoothed and polished again, would have died right there in their tracks if they had heard a rock given a voice and praising the Lord.

Well, we have great churches and we have beautiful sanctuaries and we join in the chorus, "We have need of nothing." But there is every indication that we are in need of worshipers.

We have a lot of men willing to sit on our church boards who have no desire for spiritual joy and radiance and who never show up for the church prayer meeting. These are the men who often make the decisions about the church budget and the church expenses and where the frills will go in the new edifice.

They are the fellows who run the church, but you cannot get them to the prayer meeting because they are not worshipers.

Perhaps you do not think this is an important matter, but that puts you on the other side as far as I am concerned.

It seems to me that it has always been a frightful incongruity that men who do not pray and do not worship are nevertheless actually running many of the churches and ultimately determining the direction they will take.

It hits very close to our own situations, perhaps, but we should confess that in many "good" churches, we let the women do the praying and let the men do the voting.

Because we are not truly worshipers, we spend a lot of time in the churches just spinning our wheels, burning the gasoline, making a noise but not getting anywhere.

Oh, brother or sister, God calls us to worship, but in many instances we are in entertainment, just running a poor second to the theaters.

That is where we are, even in the evangelical churches, and I don't mind telling you that most of the people we say we are trying to reach will never come to a church to see a lot of amateur actors putting on a home talent show.

I tell you, outside of politics there is not another field of activity that has more words and fewer deeds, more wind and less rain.

What are we going to do about this awesome, beautiful worship that God calls for? I would rather worship God than do any other thing I know of in all this wide world.

I would not even attempt to tell you how many hymnbooks are piled up in my study. I cannot sing a lick, but that is nobody's business. God thinks I am an opera star!

God listens while I sing to Him the old French hymns in translation, the old Latin hymns in translation. God listens while I sing the old Greek hymns from the Eastern church as well as the beautiful psalms done in meter and some of the simpler songs of Watts and Wesley and the rest.

I mean it when I say that I would rather worship God than to do anything else. You may reply, "If you worship God you do nothing else."

But that only reveals that you have not done your homework. The beautiful part of worship is that it prepares you and enables you to zero in on the important things that must be done for God.

Listen to me! Practically every great deed done in the church of Christ all the way back to the apostle Paul was done by people blazing with the radiant worship of their God.

A survey of church history will prove that it was those who were the yearning worshipers who also became the great workers. Those great saints whose hymns we so tenderly sing were active in their faith to the point that we must wonder how they ever did it all.

The great hospitals have grown out of the hearts of worshiping men. The mental institutions grew out of the hearts of worshiping and compassionate men and women. We should say, too, that wherever the church has come out of her lethargy, rising from her sleep and into the tides of revival and spiritual renewal, always the worshipers were back of it.

We will be making a mistake if we just stand back and say, "But if we give ourselves to worship, no one will do anything."

On the contrary, if we give ourselves to God's call to worship, everyone will do more than he or she is doing now. Only, what he or she does will have significance and meaning to it. It will have the quality of eternity in it—it will be gold, silver, and precious stones, not wood, hay, and stubble.

Why should we be silent about the wonders of God? We should gladly join Isaac Watts in one of his worship hymns:

> Bless, O my soul, the living God,
> Call home thy thoughts that roam abroad,
> That all the powers within me join
> In work and worship so divine.
>
> Bless, O my soul, the God of grace,
> His favors claim thy highest praise.
> Why should the wonders He has wrought
> Be lost in silence, and forgot?
>
> Let the whole earth His power confess,
> Let the whole earth adore His grace.
> The Gentiles, with the Jews, shall join
> In work and worship so divine.

I cannot speak for you, but I want to be among those who worship. I do not want just to be a part of some great ecclesiastical machine where the pastor turns the crank and the machine runs. You know—the pastor loves everybody and everybody loves him. He has to do it. He is paid to do it.

I wish that we might get back to worship again. Then when people come into the church, they will instantly sense that they have come among holy people, God's people. They can testify, "Of a truth, God is in this place."

FAILING GOD

So I tell you this, and insist on it in the Lord, that you must no longer live as the Gentiles do, in the futility of their thinking. They are darkened in their understanding and separated from the life of God because of the ignorance that is in them due to the hardening of their hearts.

EPHESIANS 4:17–18

M any people who feel they were "born into the church," and many who just take for granted their church traditions, never stop to ask, "Why do we do what we do in the church and call it worship?"

It appears they have very little knowledge of, and probably even less appreciation for, the kind of Christian believers whom Peter describes as "a royal priesthood, an holy nation, a peculiar people."

Let me ask, then, the question so many men and women with religious backgrounds never get around to asking. *What is the*

*real definition of the Christian church? What are the basic purposes
for its existence?*

Now, let me answer. I believe a local church exists to do
corporately what each Christian believer should be doing individually—and that is to worship God. It is to show forth the
excellencies of Him who has called us out of darkness into His
marvelous light. It is to reflect the glories of Christ ever shining
upon us through the ministries of the Holy Spirit.

I am going to say something to you which will sound strange.
It even sounds strange to me as I say it, because we are not used
to hearing it within our Christian fellowships. *We are saved to
worship God.* All that Christ has done for us in the past and all
that He is doing now leads to this one end. If we are denying this
truth and if we are saying that worship is not really important,
we can blame our attitudes for the great wave of arrested development in our Christian fellowships. Why should the church
of Jesus Christ be a spiritual school where hardly anyone ever
graduates from the first grade?

You know the old joke about the man asked if he was well
educated. "I should be," he answered. "I spent five years in the
fourth grade." There is no humor in the confession of any man
or woman that he or she should be a good Christian, having
spent the last nineteen years in the second and third grades of
the Christian fellowship. When did anyone ever find in the
Scriptures that the Christian church is dedicated to the prop-
osition that everyone ought to remain static? Whence came the
notion that if you are a Christian and in the fold by faith you
need never grow? On what authority are we not to worry about
Christian maturity and spiritual development?

Ask people in church why they were converted and you will get the answer: "So we could be happy, happy, happy! Everyone who is happy say Amen!" This condition is not isolated. It is the same all over North America and far beyond. I suppose all around the world we are seriously busy evangelizing and making more first graders. It seems to be a bright and accepted idea that we can keep converts in the first grade until the Lord comes, and then He will give them rule over five cities.

Now, you who know me well know that I have not said these things about the church in an effort to be clever or to make fun of the church. Certainly I have not said them in any effort to appear "holier than thou." We live in a time when the Spirit of God is saying to us, "How genuine are your concerns for lost men and women? How real are your prayers of concern for the church of Christ and its testimony to the world? How much agony of soul do you feel about the pressures of this life and modern society as they relate to the spiritual well-being of your own family?" We will do great harm to the church and to those for whom we have love and concern if we do not recognize the kind of terrible day in which we live. Are you foolish enough to believe and expect that everything is going to remain just as it was, week after week, month after month, year after year?

We all are probably better acquainted with Canadian and American and British history than with that of the rest of the world. But it is well to remember the history and the fate of Rome. One of the most civilized empires the world has known, Rome went down like a great rotten tree. She still had military strength and the show of power on the outside. But Rome had crumbled away on the inside. Rome doted on plenty of food and drink and on circuses and pleasure and, of course, on unbridled lust and immorality. What great army put the Roman Empire down? Rome fell before the barbarous hordes from the north—the Lombard, the Hun, the Ostrogoth—people who were not worthy even to care for the shoes of the Romans. Rome had become fat and weak and careless and unconcerned. And Rome died. The Roman Empire in the west ended when the last emperor, Romulus Augustulus, was deposed in AD 476. The tragedy that happened to Rome on the inside is the same kind of threat that can harm and endanger a complacent and worldly church on the inside. It is hard for a proud, unconcerned church to function as a spiritual, mature, and worshiping church. There is always the imminent danger of failure before God.

Many people loyal to the church and to forms and traditions deny that Christianity is showing any injury in our day. But it is the *internal* bleeding that brings death and decay. We may be defeated in the hour when we bleed too much within. Remember God's expectations of the Christian church, of the believers who form the invisible body of Christ. It was never in God's revealed plan that the Christian churches would degenerate to the point that they would begin functioning as social clubs. The fellowship of the saints that the Bible advises is never dependent upon the variety of social connections which the churches lean upon in these modern times. The Christian church was never intended to function as a current events forum. God did not intend for a popular news magazine to serve as a textbook, providing the ramp from which a secular discussion can take off and become airborne.

You may have heard me talk about dramatics and acting, of

make-believe and hypocrisy. If so, you are not surprised when I declare without equivocation that the church of Jesus Christ was never intended to become a religious theater. When we build a sanctuary and dedicate it to the worship of God, are we then obligated to provide a place in the church for entertainers to display their amateur talents?

I cannot believe that the holy, loving, sovereign God who has given us a plan of eternal salvation based on the sufferings and the death of our Lord Jesus Christ can be pleased when His church becomes any of these things. We are neither holy enough nor wise enough to argue against the many statements in the Bible setting forth God's expectations of His people, the church, the body of Christ. Peter reminds us that if we are believers who treasure the work of Christ on our behalf, we are a chosen generation, a royal priesthood, a holy nation, a special and peculiar people in God's sight. Paul told the Athenians that an effective and obedient believer and child of God lives and moves and has his or her being in God. If we are willing to confess that we have been called out of darkness to show forth the glory of Him who called us, we should also be willing to take whatever steps are necessary to fulfill our high design and calling as the New Testament Church. To do less than this is to fail utterly. It is to fail our God. It is to fail our Lord Jesus Christ who has redeemed us. It is to fail ourselves and to fail our children. It is also to miserably fail the Holy Spirit of God who has come from the heart of Jesus to do in us the works that can only be accomplished for God by a holy and sanctified people.

In this total concept of the Christian church and the members who compose it, there are two ways in which we can fail

God. We can disappoint Him as a church, losing our corporate witness. Generally linked with that is our failure as individual Christians. We look around at one another and use one of the oldest of all arguments: "Well, that kind of failure certainly could not happen here, among us." If we are concerned and praying Christians, we will remember a pattern. When a church weakens in any generation, failing to carry out the purposes of God, it will depart from the faith altogether in the next generation. That is how declension comes in the church. That is how apostasy comes. That is how the fundamentals of the faith are neglected. That is how the liberal and uncertain views concerning sound Christian doctrine surface. It is a serious and tragic matter that a church can actually fail. The point of failure will come when it is no longer a Christian church. The believers who remain will know that the glory has departed.

In Israel's days of journeying, God gave the visible cloud by day and the fire by night as a witness and an evidence of His glory and constant protection. If God was still giving the same signals of His abiding Presence, I wonder how many churches would have the approving cloud by day and fire by night. If you have any spiritual perception at all, I need not state that in our generation and in every community, large or small, there are churches existing merely as monuments of what they used to be. The glory has departed. The witness of God and of salvation and of eternal life is now just an uncertain sound. The monument is there, but the church has failed. God does not expect us to give up, to give in, to accept the church as it is and to condone what is happening. He expects His believing children to measure the church against the standards and the blessings promised in the

Word of God. Then, with love and reverence and prayer and in the leading of the Spirit of God, we will quietly and patiently endeavor to align the church with the Word of God. When this begins to happen, and the Word of God is given its place of priority, the presence of the Holy Spirit will again begin to glow in the church. That is what my heart longs to see.

Now, the second thing is the matter of individuals who are failing God. God has had His own purposes in the creation of every man and every woman. God wants us to know the new birth from above. He wants us to know the meaning of our salvation. He wants us to be filled with His Spirit. He wants us to know the meaning of worship. He wants us to reflect the glory of the One who has called us into His marvelous light. If we fail in this respect, then it would have been better had we never been born! The facts are plain: there is no turning back. After we are born from above, there is no turning back. We are responsible, we are accountable. How utterly tragic to be a barren fig tree, having the outward show of leaves and growth but never producing any fruit! How terrible to know that God intended us to mirror His beautiful light and to have to confess that we are shattered and useless, reflecting nothing!

Be sure we will be aware of our loss, my friend. We will be aware of it. The most startling and frightful thing about us as human beings is the eternal consciousness that God has given us. It is an awareness, a consciousness, a sensitivity given us by God Himself. It is a gift to humanity—an awareness, an ability to feel. If we had not been given such an awareness, nothing would harm us, for we would never be aware of it. Hell would not be hell if it were not for the awareness God has given men and women. If humans were just to sleep through hell, hell certainly would not be hell.

My Christian brother or sister, thank God always for the blessed gifts of sensitivity and conscience and human choice He has given you. Are you being faithful as a Christian believer where He has placed you? If God has called you out of darkness into His light, you should be worshiping Him. If He has shown you that you are to show forth the excellencies, the virtues, the beauties of the Lord who has called you, then you should be humbly and gladly worshiping Him with the radiance and the blessing of the Holy Spirit in your life.

It is sad that we humans do not always function joyfully for God in the place He has marked out for us. We may even allow trifling things and minor incidents to disturb our fellowship with God and our spiritual witness for Him who is our Savior.

I once had an opportunity to preach in another pulpit, and after the service I was seated in a restaurant with the pastor. A man came by our table with his wife, and they stopped for a moment to talk. "I enjoyed hearing you today, Mr. Tozer," he said. "It was like old times." There were tears in his eyes and a softness in his voice as he recalled a minor incident in our church life years before. "I just foolishly walked out, and today was a reminder of what I have been missing," he said. He then excused himself, and the couple bade us goodbye.

The man was fully aware of the consequences of poor choices and snap judgments apart from the leading of God's Spirit. I know very well that he was not talking about my sermon or my preaching. He was talking about faithfulness to the Word of God. He was talking about the sweet and satisfying fellowship among those who love the Lord. He was talking about the loss of something intrinsic and beautiful which only comes to us in our obedience to God's revealed truth.

There is no limit to what God can do through us if we are His yielded and purified people, worshiping and showing forth His glory and His faithfulness. We must have an awareness, also, of what sin and uncleanness are doing all around us. Sin does not recognize any kind of borders or limits. Sin does not operate exclusively in the ghettos. Wherever you are, in the suburbs or in the country, sin is sin. And wherever there is sin, the devil rages, and demons are abroad.

In this kind of a sinful world, what are you doing with the spiritual light and awareness God has given you? Where do you stand with God in your friendships, in your pleasures, in the complexities of your day-to-day life? The psychologists have been telling us for some time now that we will not have so many problems if we can just get to the place where we do not let our religion "bother" us. We are told we can dispel most of our personal problems by shedding our guilt complexes. I am thankful that God has made us with an eternal awareness, and that He knows how to lay the proper care and concern upon us.

People call on me for spiritual guidance and counseling. But I can do little for them. When a person has come to the place of submission and obedience, God has promised that He will give that person all the comfort he or she needs.

After my arrival in Toronto, a cultured, attractive young woman made an appointment to see me in my office. When she came, we talked for a few moments to get acquainted, and then she came to the point. She said she was troubled about her homosexual relations with her roommate. She told me she had already talked with other professionals about this. I had the distinct impression she hoped I would assure her that what she was doing was permissible in our day. Instead, I faced her squarely. "Young woman," I said, "you are guilty of sodomy, and God is not going to give you any approval or comfort until you turn from your known sin and seek His forgiveness and cleansing."

"I guess I needed to hear that," she admitted.

As a Christian minister and counselor, there was no way that I could console and comfort that girl and ease and soften the pain of guilt she was experiencing within her being. She would have to endure it until the moment of decision when she would confess her sin and plunge by faith into that cleansing fountain filled with blood from Immanuel's veins.

That is the remedy, that is the comfort and the necessary strength God has promised to those whose awareness and sensitivity lead them to repentance and forgiveness and wholeness. God assures us in many ways that His worshiping people will be a purified people, a people delighting in the spiritual disciplines of a life pleasing to God. No person who has found the blessings of purity and joy in the Holy Spirit can ever be defeated. No church that has discovered the delight and satisfaction of adoring worship that springs automatically from love and obedience to God can ever perish.

3

THE REASON
WE EXIST

Let the king be enthralled by your beauty;
honor him, for he is your lord.

PSALM 45:11

G od made us to worship. That is why we were created. Everything has its reason for being here. We have this reason:
that we might worship the Father Almighty, Maker of heaven
and earth. And we sinned and lost the glory and fell, and the
light went out in our hearts, and we stopped worshiping God.
And set out affections on things below.

But God sent His only begotten Son. He was born of the
virgin Mary, suffered under Pontius Pilate, was crucified, dead
and buried, and rose the third day from the dead. And He sitteth
at the right hand of the Majesty in the heavens in order that He
might restore us again to worship. Indeed, not only restore us
again to worship, but put as much higher as Christ is higher than
Adam. For all we could do in Adam was to be equal to Adam,

but in Christ, He raises us up until we shall be like Him. So that actually redemption is an improvement upon creation. . . .

He redeems us that we might worship again, that we might take our place again, even on earth with the angels in heaven, and the beasts and the living creatures. That we might feel in our hearts and express in our own way that humbling but nevertheless delightful sense of admiring awe and astonished wonder and overwhelming love—in the presence of that ancient mystery, that unspeakable majesty, that Ancient of Days. And I want you to notice that I said "that . . . that . . . that." Why did I not say "He"? Because the human heart in its present state, in the presence of mystery, always says some*thing* before it says some*one*. In 1 John, the Holy Ghost says,

> That which was from the beginning, which we have heard, which we have seen with our eyes, which we have looked upon, and our hands have handled, of the Word of life; (For the life was manifested, and we have seen it, and bear witness, and shew unto you that eternal life, which was with the Father, and was manifested unto us;) That which we have seen and heard declare we unto you. (1 John 1:1–3)

Now that was an inspired apostle speaking, and he said, "that . . . that . . . that . . . which," not "who . . . whom . . . He." In the presence of the overarching mystery, the human heart reaches up and leans out and feels and says something. And it always says something before it can say someone.

Why did John say "that" instead of "He"? Because at the root of human thought there is an *it*. At the root of human thought there is *that*. And the human heart searches for the original substance, for being, for empathy.

The little word *esse* in Latin means "to be" or "actual being." It is this that the human heart struggles for. In the midst of the whirling waters of humanity and sin and time and space, man's heart struggles for the rock of being, the rock of *esse*, the essential, the actual being. And our fathers knew that when they talked about the substance or essence of God, or when they said that the Son was the essence of the Father, or when they said that the Spirit was the same essence of the Father and the Son.

The first thrust of the human heart is for that rock of being where He says, "that which was with the Father." As we reason and pray, and read and meditate on the Word of God, "that" becomes "He." And Jesus says, "After this manner therefore pray ye: Our Father which art in heaven. . ." (Matt. 6:9).

There lived once, in the 17th century, a man by the name of Blaise Pascal. Pascal was probably the greatest mind in the 17th century, and I personally think the greatest mind France ever produced, although I'm probably not in a position to pronounce on that. It would take a great deal of scholarship to say for certain. But this man goes down in history and is found in all books and in the encyclopedias and in the histories of science and mathematics as probably the greatest thinker of the 17th century. He was a scientist, he was a mathematician, and he was a philosopher. He didn't write much, but what he wrote has been seminal. It has come like the seed of God in the minds of men. Well this man astonished the learned world by his work on mathematics, particularly geometry, when he was only in his early twenties. But later on, Pascal became interested in theology and then found God and became a Christian. And while he went on with his scientific work, he began to write about God and Christ and redemption and revelation. He wrote with such wondrous clarity and insight that he startled the learned of the universities of his time.

Pascal wrote a little testimony, and he folded that testimony up and put it in close to his heart, and all his life he carried it here, close to his heart. Now this is only part of it. It isn't very long, but I'm giving you only part of it. A little of it's written in Latin, and the rest of it is translated into English. Here it is: Pascal says, "From about half past ten at night to about half after midnight, fire…" Cuts it off there. Doesn't go on. Just cuts it off and then prays, "Oh God of Abraham, God of Isaac, God of Jacob, not of the philosophers nor the wise. Security, security, feeling, joy, peace, the God Jesus Christ shall be my God."

Imagine one of the greatest minds of the last thousand years carrying this against his heart. Forgetfulness of the world and of all save God, he can be found only in the ways taught in the gospel. "Oh, righteous Father, the world hath not known Thee, but I have known Thee. Joy, joy, joy, joy, tears of joy." He kept that against his heart while he studied the heavens and wrote his great books. But he repudiated the god of the thinker and of the philosopher and sought the God and Father of our Lord Jesus Christ, who can be found only in the ways of the gospel. "Fire, fire," he said, "from ten thirty to twelve thirty. For His sake I repudiate the world." . . .

In Luke 2:11, the angel said, "For unto you is born this day in the city of David a Saviour, which is Christ the Lord." Now comes the bliss and wonder of revelation and manifestation. And to the thirsting, searching mind that is crying for "that" and "it" and substance and essence and being, the angels sing. He is thy Lord. Worship thou Him.

Now God has given us this object of our worship. He is person, but He is also being. He is one, but He is also *that*—that ancient mystery, that unutterable majesty in whose presence angels tremble, and the creatures who have gazed for centuries on the sea of fire fold their wings and cry, "Holy, holy, holy, is the LORD of hosts" (Isa. 6:3).

I want to discuss only two things of which He is Lord.

He is Lord of all, and you'll find that over in the book of Acts. "He is Lord of all!" said the man, Peter (Acts 10:36). And He is the Lord of all being. What I've said is just as orthodox as Augustine and just as evangelical as Dwight Moody. So don't imagine that because I'm using language that you may not be familiar with that I'm off the deep end somewhere. He is Lord of all being. That is, He is not the Lord of all beings. That would have been a cheap way to say it. Lord of all beings is a kind of a boss over the beings. No, He's that, but that wasn't what the man meant or said. He is the Lord of all being. He is Lord of the concept of being. He is the Lord of all possibility of being. He is that, and that is He. And He is the Lord of all actual existence, and He is the Lord.

And so, my friends, when we worship Him, we encompass all science and all philosophy. Science is great, philosophy is greater, theology is greater still, and worship is greatest of all. For worship goes back of where science can go, back of where human thought can penetrate, back of all the wordings of theology, and back to the reality. And when the Christian gets on his knees, he is having a meeting at the summit. He can't get beyond that. There isn't an archangel that can go higher than he can go. There isn't a cherub that can burn his way higher than he can go, for he is worshiping that awful mystery, that overwhelming majesty in humbling but delightful love. He's worshiping his God.

And so I tell you that when we are called as Christians, we are not simply called to give up only a few little things and saved from doing a few bad things. Giving all up will come with the Christian's new birth. He has been born again that he might push through and press in past the blood-sprinkled way and find that after which the minds of men sought and seek.

I remember when an old man came down from the hills of Tishbi dressed in camel's hair and girded about the loins with a leather girdle. He had never seen a king, and a palace was unknown to him. The pine trees had been his temple, and the sound of the wind had been his organ. And the stars at night had spoken to him and whispered of the Lord God of his fathers. And he knew the Word, but he walked boldly into the presence of a degenerate, decadent king and said, "I am Elijah. I stand before God." He was bored with royal red tape, bored with scepters and crowns and cheap little barber chairs set up and called thrones. He was bored and essentially said, "I've spent my year standing in the presence of the Ancient of Days, and I'm not afraid of kings. I come with a message: there will be no rain." Then he disappeared, walking with rustic dignity out of the presence of that puppet king. A cheap utensil used by a Baalitish woman called Jezebel.

So when the whole world exploded, "Oh! They've sent up a satellite!" Well, they're good at satellites. They've got a lot of them.

And I'm bored with it. I've stood in the presence of Him who encompasses the universes and holds them in His hand. He calleth the stars by name and leadeth them forth, as a shepherd leads forth his sheep, across the blue-green heavens above. Now am I therefore going to fall down and worship and say how wonderful? I worship the Lord of the sun and the stars and of all space and all time, and of all matter and of all motion. Therefore, I am not too excited. He is the Lord of all being, not of the philosophers and not of the wise man. But the revealed God; the God that reveals Himself; the God of Abraham, Isaac, and Jacob; the God and Father of our Lord Jesus Christ. And since He is the God of all being, He is the enemy of all not-being. Therefore, when some fellow with a highly illustrated book rushes up your sidewalk and wants to play you a little disc, shut the door—kindly, like a Christian, but shut it, for he wants to talk to you about annihilation. There's no such concept in the Bible as annihilation. The Lord of all being is the enemy of all not-being. And God knows nothing of not-being. He knows only being.

He is also the Lord of life. And again, I turn to John:

That which was from the beginning, which we have heard, which we have seen with our eyes, which we have looked upon, and our hands have handled, of the Word of life; (For the life was manifested, and we have seen it, and bear witness, and shew unto you that eternal life, which was with the Father, and was manifested unto us;) That which we have seen and heard declare we unto you, that ye also may have fellowship with us: and truly our fellowship is with the Father, and with his Son Jesus Christ. (1 John 1:1–3)

So there He is the Father of all life. "He is the Lord of all," said Peter (Acts 10:36). "He is thy Lord. Worship thou Him!" said David (Ps. 45:11). He is of life, the sole fountain. There isn't any other life, and He is the fountain of that life. All the light we know comes from the sun. That is all we know. I suppose the stars give off light and all that, but we're thinking as plain people now, looking up at the sun. All light comes from the sun, and so all life comes from God and Jesus Christ, the Son. And when the man of God said, "Thou of life the fountain art / Freely let me take of Thee," he was like Elijah on the mountains of Tishbi. He'd gone past Shakespeare and past Homer, he'd gone past all the philosophers and the wise and was worshiping in the presence of the Lord of all life.

> Thou of life the fountain art,
> Freely let me take of Thee;
> Spring Thou up within my heart;
> Rise to all eternity.

You can go into the average library, and you will not find anything as magnificent as those four lines. The books and the plays and all the celebrities—they all stop when the undertaker comes. This man says, "Spring Thou up within my heart; rise to all eternity." When the stars have faded out, and all the suns have burnt themselves away, we'll still be with Him. For He is the Lord of life, He is the Lord of the essence of life, He is the Lord of all the possibility of life, He's the Lord of all kinds of life, and there is no life that is not from Him. And since He is the Lord of life, He is the enemy of death.

But now is Christ risen from the dead, and become the firstfruits of them that slept. For since by man came death, by man came also the resurrection of the dead. For as in Adam all die, even so in Christ shall all be made alive. But every man in his own order: Christ the firstfruits; afterward they that are Christ's at his coming.

Then cometh the end, when he shall have delivered up the kingdom to God, even the Father; when he shall have put down all rule and all authority and power. For he must reign, till he hath put all enemies under his feet. The last enemy that shall be destroyed is death. (1 Cor. 15:20–26)

Since He is the Lord of life, He is the enemy of death. And He came down and went into this cave, where death snarled and snapped its jaws, and went in there with it in the darkness. We called it a cross on a hill, but it was a cave where a snarling dragon lay. He broke its filthy jaw and rose again the third day. He threw its teeth in all directions, which would never be gathered together again. He is the enemy of death—the enemy of my death and the enemy of yours. He is the Lord of life.

What does that mean to us? I ran into this written by an old German:

> Jesus lives, and so shall I.
> Death! thy sting is gone forever!
> He who deigned for me to die,
> Lives, the bands of death to sever.
> He shall raise me from the dust:
> Jesus is my Hope and Trust.

That is what it means. Jesus lives, and death is now but an entrance into glory.

> Courage, then, my soul, for thou
> Hast a crown of life before thee;
> Thou shalt find thy hopes were just;
> Jesus is the Christian's Trust.

The old brother who wrote this was evangelical and evangelistic. He couldn't close his hymn without giving the poor sinner outside a chance to come in. So he said Jesus lives and God extends His grace to each returning sinner. He receives rebels as friends and exalts them to the highest honor. God is true as He is just; Jesus is my hope and trust.

That's what it's all about, my brethren. I wish the world could hear it. I'd like to tell it to the whole world. I'd like to have it circulated. I'd like these ideas to get a hold of the minds of men until a new day would dawn in evangelical circles.

I remember that John Keats said, "I have fears that I may cease to be before my pen has glean'd my teeming brain." And he did. The teeming brain into which he dipped his pen and wrote his imperishable poems darkened at twenty-four.

And the same Pascal from whom I have quoted, "Fire, fire, joy, joy, tears of joy," said, "I'm going to write so that the world will get it." I'd like to be able to make my voice heard all over the world to the poor, poor church living on cheap fiction, living on the smiles and bows of converted celebrities, living to sing cheap songs about, "Once I smoked, now I don't. Once I drank beer, now I don't." Thank God you don't, brother. It's cheaper not to—and healthier. But if that's your concept of Christianity, you haven't even seen the door of the outer chambers, let alone the Holy of Holies or the sanctum sanctorum.

Let's push all in. Let's tell the world why He died and why He lives! That a people once made to worship Him who had lost their harp and lost their tongue and lost their desire even to worship are now caught and renewed and made alive and able to worship again. And it works, my brethren. It works.

In 1935, a man named Jeffery moved from Indo-China to a country called Borneo. There he found headhunters, men with poisoned arrows which they shot through blow guns. And they'd hunt those heads, shrink them and hang them up. And he went in there and prayed through and almost died one night. But praying through, God began to work. The headhunters began to get converted, and men all over that area began to get converted. They built their chapels, they threw their idols away, and with joy, they gathered up these shrunken heads and threw them into the river that carried them out into the sea.

Now in their language they talk about "Yesu," Jesus Christ the Son of God. It works, my brethren. He saved them from head-hunting. But it's not just what he saved them from, it's what he saved them to! To kneel in a simple bamboo chapel and worship the Lord God Almighty, Maker of heaven and earth, and Jesus Christ His only Son. That's what he saved them to! And that's all that matters.

Jesus lives and offers to returning sinners a place in His heart. He might restring your harp and give you back your organ— your organ that can play the anthems and join with the hosts above. Dear God, how far the church has wandered, and how far we all are from being the kind of Christians we ought to be. Put away fleshly things. Put away worldly things. Put away the cheap twaddle of fallen Adam's brood. Turn your eyes onto Jesus, the Lamb of God. Your mind and heart will be cleansed. Trust the Holy Ghost to fill your heart and spirit with worship again, so you may join the angels and all the redeemed—the prophets and saints and martyrs—in singing the songs of the Father, and the Son who bled for you, and the Holy Ghost who is the Spirit of the Father and the Son.

TRUE WORSHIP REQUIRES THE NEW BIRTH

But because of his great love for us, God, who is rich in mercy, made us alive with Christ even when we were dead in transgressions—it is by grace you have been saved.

EPHESIANS 2:4–5

There are many weird ideas about God in our day, and therefore there are all kinds of substitutes for true worship. Often I have heard someone or another within the Christian church confess sadly: "I guess I don't really know very much about God." If that is a true confession, the man or woman should then be honest enough to make a necessarily parallel confession: "I guess I don't really know very much about worship." Actually, basic beliefs about the person and the nature of God have changed so much that there are among us now men and women who find it easy to brag about the benefits they receive from God—without ever a thought or a desire to know the true meaning of worship!

I have immediate reactions to such an extreme misunderstanding of the true nature of a holy and sovereign God. My first is that I believe the very last thing God desires is to have shallow-minded and worldly Christians bragging about Him. My second is that it does not seem to be very well recognized that God's highest desire is that every one of His believing children should so love and so adore Him that we are continuously in His presence, in Spirit and in truth.

That is to worship, indeed. Something wonderful and miraculous and life-changing takes place within the human soul when Jesus Christ is invited in to take His rightful place. That is exactly what God anticipated when He wrought the plan of salvation. He intended to make worshipers out of rebels; He intended to restore to men and women the place of worship which our first parents knew when they were created.

If we know this result as a blessed reality in our own lives and experience, then it is evident that we are not just waiting for Sunday to come so we can "go to church and worship."

True worship of God must be a constant and consistent attitude or state of mind within the believer. It will always be a sustained and blessed acknowledgement of love and adoration, subject in this life to degrees of perfection and intensity.

Now, the negative side of the common approach to worship needs to be stated. Contrary to much that is being said and practiced in the churches, true worship of God is not something that we "do" in the hope of appearing to be religious! No one can really argue that many people whose dearest desire is just to be numbered with those who are "sensitive to religion" place their weekly emphasis upon faithfulness in attending "the service of worship."

What do the Christian Scriptures have to say to us at this point as we consider the reality of fellowship between God and His redeemed children? What we learn is very plain and very encouraging. Having been made in His image, we have within us the capacity to know God and the instinct that we should worship Him. The very moment that the Spirit of God has quickened us to His life in regeneration, our whole being senses its kinship to God and leaps up in joyous recognition!

That response within our beings, a response to forgiveness and pardon and regeneration, signals the miracle of the heavenly birth—without which we cannot see the kingdom of God. Yes, God desires and is pleased to communicate with us through the avenues of our minds, our wills, and our emotions. The continuous and unembarrassed interchange of love and thought between God and the souls of redeemed men and women is the throbbing heart of the New Testament religion.

Actually, it is impossible to consider this new relationship without confessing that the primary work of the Holy Spirit is to restore the lost soul to intimate fellowship with God through the washing of regeneration. To accomplish this, He first reveals Christ to the penitent heart: "Wherefore I give you to understand, that no man speaking by the Spirit of God calleth Jesus accursed: and that no man can say that Jesus is the Lord, but by the Holy Ghost" (1 Cor. 12:3).

Then consider Christ's own words to His disciples concerning the brighter rays from His own being which will illuminate the newborn soul: "But the Comforter, which is the Holy Ghost, whom the Father will send in my name, he shall teach you all things, and bring all things to your remembrance, whatsoever I have said unto you" (John 14:26). Remember, we know Christ only as the Spirit enables us. How thankful we should be to discover that it is God's desire to lead every willing heart into depths and heights of divine knowledge and communion. As soon as God sends the Spirit of His Son into our hearts, we say "Abba"—and we are worshiping, but probably not in the full New Testament sense of the word.

God desires to take us deeper into Himself. We will have much to learn in the school of the Spirit. He wants to lead us on in our love for Him who first loved us. He wants to cultivate within us the adoration and admiration of which He is worthy. He wants to reveal to each of us the blessed element of spiritual fascination in true worship. He wants to teach us the wonder of being filled with moral excitement in our worship, entranced with the knowledge of who God is. He wants us to be astonished at the inconceivable elevation and magnitude and splendor of Almighty God!

There can be no human substitute for this kind of worship and for this kind of Spirit-given response to the God who is our Creator and Redeemer and Lord. There is all around us, however, a very evident and continuing substitute for worship. I speak of the compelling temptation among Christian believers to be constantly engaged, during every waking hour, in religious activity. We cannot deny that it is definitely a churchly idea of service. Many of our sermons and much of our contemporary ecclesiastical teaching lean toward the idea that it is surely God's plan for us to be busy, busy, busy—because it is the best cause in the world in which we are involved.

But if there is any honesty left in us, it persuades us in our quieter moments that true spiritual worship is at a discouragingly low ebb among professing Christians. Do we dare ask how we have reached this state? If you are willing to ask it, I am willing to try to answer it. Actually, I will answer it by asking another obvious question. How can our approach to worship be any more vital than it is when so many who lead us, both in the pulpit and in the pew, give little indication that the fellowship of God is delightful beyond telling? Think back for a moment into your New Testament knowledge, and you will have to agree that this is exactly the point that Jesus was making to the stern and self-righteous Pharisees about true worship in their day. They were religious in their daily life. They were outwardly pious and well acquainted with the forms of worship—but within their beings were attitudes and faults and hypocrisies which caused Jesus to describe them as "whitewashed sepulchers." The only righteousness they knew and understood was their own outward form of righteousness based on the maintenance of a fairly high level of external morality. Because they thought of God as being as stern and austere and unforgiving as they themselves were, their concept of worship was necessarily low and unworthy. To a Pharisee, the service of God was a bondage which he did not love but from which he could not escape without a loss too great to bear. God, as the Pharisees saw Him, was not a God easy to live with. So their daily religion became grim and hard, with no trace of true love in it.

It can be said about us, as humans, that we try to be like our God. If He is conceived to be stern and exacting and harsh, so will we be! The blessed and inviting truth is that God is the most

47

winsome of all beings, and in our worship of Him we should find unspeakable pleasure. The living God has been willing to reveal Himself to our seeking hearts. He would have us know and understand that He is all love and that those who trust Him need never know anything but that love.

God would have us know that He is just, indeed, and He will not condone sin. He has tried to make it overwhelmingly plain to us that through the blood of the everlasting covenant He is able to act toward us exactly as if we had never sinned. Unbeknown to the understanding of a Pharisee, God communes with His redeemed ones in an easy, uninhibited fellowship that is restful and healing to the soul.

The God who has redeemed us in love, through the merits of the Eternal Son, is not unreasonable. He is not selfish. Neither is He temperamental. What He is today we shall find Him tomorrow and the next day and next year.

The God who desires our fellowship and communion is not hard to please, although He may be hard to satisfy. He expects of us only what He has Himself supplied. He is quick to mark every simple effort to please Him and just as quick to overlook our imperfections when He knows we meant to do His will.

This is the best of good news: God loves us for ourselves. He values our love more than He values galaxies of new created worlds. He remembers our frame and knows that we are dust. The God we love may sometimes chasten us, it is true. But even this He does with a smile—the proud, tender smile of a Father who is bursting with pleasure over an imperfect but promising son who is coming every day to look more and more like the One whose child he is. We should revel in the joy of believing that God is the sum of all patience and the true essence of kindly good will. We please Him most, not by frantically trying to make ourselves good, but by throwing ourselves into His arms with all our imperfections and believing that He understands everything—and loves us still.

The gratifying part of all this is that the intercourse between God and the redeemed soul is known to us in conscious, personal awareness. It is a personal awareness, indeed. The awareness does not come through the body of believers, as such, but is known to the individual and to the body through the individuals composing it. And, yes, it is conscious; it does not stay below the threshold of consciousness and work there unknown to the soul.

This communication, this consciousness, is not an end but really an inception. There is the point of reality where we begin our fellowship and friendship and communion with God. But where we stop no man has yet discovered, for there is in the mysterious depths for the triune God neither limit nor end. When we come into this sweet relationship, we are beginning to learn astonished reverence, breathless adoration, awesome fascination, lofty admiration of the attributes of God and something of the breathless silence that we know when God is near.

You may never have realized it before, but all of those elements in our perception and consciousness of the divine presence add up to what the Bible calls "the fear of God." We can know a million fears in our hours of pain or in threats of danger or in the anticipation of punishment or death. What we need to plainly recognize is that the fear of God the Bible commends can never be induced by threats or punishment of any kind. The fear of God is that "astonished reverence" of which the great Faber wrote. I would say that it may grade anywhere from its basic element—the terror of the guilty soul before a holy God—to the fascinated rapture of the worshiping saint. There are very few unqualified things in our lives, but I believe that the reverential fear of God mixed with love and fascination and astonishment and admiration and devotion is the most enjoyable state and the most purifying emotion the human soul can know.

In my own being, I could not exist very long as a Christian without this inner consciousness of the presence and nearness of God. I guess there are some persons who find themselves strong enough to live day-by-day on the basis of ethics without any intimate spiritual experience. They say Benjamin Franklin was such a man. He was a deist and not a Christian. Whitefield prayed for him and told him he was praying for him, but Franklin said, "I guess it is not doing any good because I am not saved yet." This is what Franklin did. He kept a daily graph on a series of little square charts which represented such virtues as honesty, faithfulness, charity, and probably a dozen others. He worked these into a kind of calendar, and when he had violated one of the virtues, he would write it down. When he had gone for a day or a month without having broken any of his self-imposed commandments, he considered that he was doing pretty well as a human being. A sense of ethics? Yes. Any sense of the divine? No. No mystical overtone. No worship. No reverence. No fear of God before his eyes. All of this according to his own testimony.

I do not belong to that breed of man. I can only keep right by keeping the fear of God on my soul and delighting in the fascinated rapture of worship. Apart from that, I do not know any rules at all. I am sorry that this powerful sense of godly fear is a missing quality in the churches today, and its absence is a portent and a sign. It should hover over us like the cloud over Israel. It should lie upon us like a sweet, invisible mantle. It should be a force in the conditioning of our inner lives. It should provide extra meaning for every text of Scripture. It should be making every day of the week a holy day and every spot of ground we tread holy ground. We continue to shake from our own kinds of fears: fear of Communism, fear of the collapse of civilization, even the fear of invasion from some other planet. Men think they know what fear means. But we are talking about the awe and the reverence of a loving and holy God. That kind of a fear of God is a spiritual thing and can only be brought by the presence of God.

When the Holy Spirit came at Pentecost, there was a great fear upon all the people, yet they were not afraid of anything! A child of God, made perfect in love, has no fear because perfect love casts out fear. Yet he or she is the person of all persons who most fears God.

Take the apostle John as an illustration. When Jesus was arrested in the garden, John was among those who ran away. Probably he was afraid of being arrested and put into jail. That was his fear of danger, fear of punishment, fear of humiliation. But later the same John, exiled on Patmos for the testimony of Jesus Christ, saw an awesome man standing amid the golden lampstands. The Man was clothed in a white robe and girded with a golden girdle. His feet were like burnished brass, and a sword proceeded from His mouth. His hair was as white as snow, and His face shone like the sun in its strength. The awe and reverence and fascination and fear suddenly concentrated so completely in

John's being that he could only fall unconscious to the ground. Then this holy Priest, whom he later found was Jesus Christ Himself, bearing the keys of death and hell, came and lifted John up and brought life back into him. Now, John was not afraid, and he did not feel threatened. He was experiencing a different kind of fear, a godly fear. It was a holy thing, and John felt it.

The presence of God in our midst—bringing a sense of godly fear and reverence—this is largely missing today. You cannot induce it by soft organ music and light streaming through beautifully designed windows. You cannot induce it by holding up a biscuit and claiming that it is God. You cannot induce it by any kind or any amount of mumbo-jumbo. What people feel in the presence of that kind of paganism is not the true fear of God. It is just the inducement of a superstitious dread. A true fear of God is a beautiful thing, for it is worship, it is love, it is veneration. It is a high moral happiness because God is. It is a delight so great that if God were not, the worshiper would not want to be, either. He or she could easily pray, "My God, continue to be as Thou art, or let me die! I cannot think of any other God but Thee!"

True worship is to be so personally and hopelessly in love with God that the idea of a transfer of affection never even remotely exists. That is the meaning of the fear of God. Because worship is largely missing, do you know what we are doing? We are doing our best to sew up that rent veil in the temple. We use artificial means to try to induce some kind of worship. I think the devil in hell must be laughing, and I think God must be grieving, for there is no fear of God before our eyes.

5

WORSHIP AS HE WILLS

*God is spirit, and his worshipers must
worship in the Spirit and in truth.*

JOHN 4:24

G od wants us to worship Him. The devil, or our own unbe-
lieving minds, would like to tell us that God does not particularly want us to worship Him—we owe it to Him, but that
God isn't concerned. But the truth is God wants us to worship
Him. We're not unwanted children. God wants us to worship
Him, I repeat. Why was it that when God came in the cool of
the day to talk with Adam, He couldn't find Adam and cried,
"Adam, where art thou?" God seeking worship from an Adam
who had sinned.

And our Lord in Luke 4 says, "Thou shalt worship the Lord
thy God, and Him only shalt thou serve." It's not only desired
that we worship God, but He has commanded us to do it. And
have you noticed in Psalm 45, "So shall the king greatly desire

thy beauty" (v. 11)? God finds something in us. It is something that He put there. But it's there.

My friend, there are several kinds of unbelief, or rather several phases or facets to unbelief. One of them is that we don't think we're as bad as God says we are. And if we don't have faith in God's Word concerning our badness, we'll never repent. Then there is another facet of faith. It is this: that we don't believe that we are as dear to God as He says we are. And we don't believe that He desires us as much as He says He does. If everybody could suddenly have a baptism of pure, cheerful belief that God wanted me and that God wanted me to worship Him and that God wanted me to pray and admire Him and praise Him, it could transform our Christian fellowship and change us overnight into the most radiantly happy people.

"So shall the king greatly desire thy beauty: for he is thy Lord; and worship thou him."

And it's written in 2 Thessalonians about when Jesus shall come to be glorified in His saints and be admired by all who believe (1:10). That is, God is admired, not the people admired. And the whole import and substance of the New Testament—of all the Bible, really—is that God made us to worship Him, and when we're not worshiping Him, we're failing in the purpose for which we were created. That we're stars without light and sun without heat and clouds without water and birds without song and harps without music. We simply are failing and falling short.

I want to be very clear that we cannot worship Him as we will. The One who made us to worship Him has also decreed how we should worship Him. God does not accept just any kind of worship. He accepts worship only when it is pure and when it is inspired by the Holy Ghost. You see, God has rejected almost all of the worship of mankind in our present condition. Though God wants us to worship Him and commands us to and asks us to, and obviously was anxious and hurt when Adam failed to worship Him, yet nevertheless God condemns and rejects almost all the worship of mankind for reasons which I am going to show you. Let us break up the worship of man, the rejected worship, the worship that God won't receive. Let us break it up into Cain worship, Samaritan worship, pagan worship, and nature worship. For there are at least those four kinds of worship that are brought in the earth, and God rejects all of them.

There's Cain's worship. I assume you're a Bible reader and you know that while Abel offered under God a sacrifice of blood, Cain offered no sacrifice of blood. He came with a bloodless sacrifice and offered flowers and fruit and of the growth of the earth to the Lord. And this attempted worship rested upon three errors.

First, it rested upon a mistaken impression of the kind of God that God is. Cain was born of fallen parents and Cain had never heard the voice of the God in the garden. And when Cain came to worship God, he came to a god other than God. He came to a god of his own imagination.

The second error was that man occupies a relation to God other than what he actually does. You see that a lot of religious people are mistaken. They assume that we humans occupy a relation to God which we do not occupy. We think we are God's children and we talk about God the Father of mankind, but the Bible does not teach that God is the Father of all mankind.

The third error is that sin is less serious than it is in fact.

Cain made all of these mistakes. He thought that God was

a different kind of god than what He is. He thought he himself was a different kind of man from what he was. And he thought that sin was less vicious and serious than God said it was. So he came cheerfully, bringing his sacrifice, and offered God worship, which we simply call "Cain worship." It was the worship without atonement.

Always keep this in mind: while God says, "He is thy Lord; worship thou Him," and while He calls, "Where art thou?" and while He commands we must worship Him in spirit and in truth, He bluntly and summarily rejects worship that is not founded on redeeming blood.

Then there's Samaritan worship. You know about the Samaritans, how under Omri and Ahab the city of Samaria became a religious center, and Jerusalem was rejected as the place. The Samaritans were heretics in the right sense of the word, because heretical doesn't always mean that we are false. A man can be a heretic and not teach anything particularly false. Did you know that? A heretic is not necessarily one who teaches that there is no Trinity or that God did not create the earth or that there is no judgment. They are heretics, too, but heresy doesn't mean "to teach wrong." The very word heretic means "one who picks and chooses." So that the Samaritans were heretics in that they chose certain parts of the Old Testament. They said, "Well, we accept the Pentateuch, but we reject David and Isaiah and Jeremiah and Ezekiel and Daniel and first and second Kings and the Song of Solomon and all the named."

And then they said, "We believe," and then they did some translating. You know how you can translate anything and prove what you're out to prove? Anybody can do that. All you have to do is to say, "I know the Greek," or "I know the Hebrew," and after that they're on their own. So they translated the old Pentateuch in a manner that made Samaria the place of worship and said, "Here, Samaria is the place of worship!" And of course, they were hostile to the Jews who said, "No. Our fathers worshiped in Jerusalem! God gave them this hill, Moriah, and here on this hill Solomon built the temple. And that is the place where people should worship." There Christ came! And they said, "No, no. We're to worship in Samaria." And yet they accepted the Pentateuch. They accepted as much of the Bible as they wanted.

I don't think I have to spell it out and mark it in red ink for you to see how much heresy there is these days—believing what we want to believe, emphasizing what we want to emphasize, and following along in one path but rejecting another, doing one thing but refusing another, and thus we become heretics because we've become pickers and choosers among the truths of God. That is Samaritan worship.

Then there's pagan worship. I could go back if I wanted and search into the worship of the early Egyptians and pagans. I do have their books! The Egyptian book of the dead and the teachings of Zoroaster and Buddha. And the laws of man. If we wanted to do it, we could make a case and preach for two weeks, if anybody would listen, about the worship of the pagans, the heathen worship.

Paul talks about it, and Paul hasn't a kind thing to say about it. He condemns it outright and says, "When they knew God, they glorified him not as God, neither were they thankful; but became vain in their imaginations, and their foolish heart was darkened" (Rom. 1:21). And down they went from God to man, and from man to bird, and from bird to beast, and from beast to fish, and from fish to creeping things that wriggle on the earth. That was man's terrible trip downward in his worship.

And then there is nature worship. I will say to you that I have more sympathy with this than I do liberalism. But at the same time, it won't do. For nature worship is but the poetry of religion. You know, religion does have a lot of poetry in it, and it properly does have and should have. We sing a lot of poetry in church, don't we? And most everybody smiles and shrugs and says, "Oh, I'm no poet, I don't care for poetry." But they do. You get a fellow excited and get him to tell you something he's seen, and then instantaneously you'll fall into metaphors and similes and figures of speech. "He's a poet," as they say, "and doesn't know it." We're all poets, and religion brings poetry out more than any occupation that the mind can be engaged in, and there is a lot that is very beautiful about religion. There is a high enjoyment in the contemplation of the divine and sublime, and the concentration of the mind upon beauty. It always brings a high sense of enjoyment.

Well, that's nature worship. And some mistake this nature worship, this rapt feeling, for true worship. You remember that Emerson, who was no Christian, said that on occasion—walking across a field at night after a rain with the sun shining on the little puddles of water out over the meadow—suddenly had his mind elevated to a place of such happiness that he was full of fear. He said, "I was so happy, I was afraid!" He was simply a pagan poet is all! And a whole lot of worship that's going on these days is nothing else but pagan poetry. It's nature worship.

Some mistake the music of religion as true worship because music elevates the mind. Music raises the heart to near rapture.

Music can lift our feelings to ecstasy. Music has a purifying, purging effect upon us. So it's possible to fall into a happy and elevated state of mind with a vague notion about God and imagine we're worshiping God when we're doing nothing of the sort. We are simply enjoying. It is that which God put in us and which sin hasn't yet been able to kill.

I don't think there's any poetry in hell. I can't believe that among the terrible sewage of the moral world, there's going to be anybody breaking into similes and metaphors and song in that terrible hell! We read about it in heaven because it belongs there. But as far as I know, in my Bible, we never hear of it in hell. We hear about conversation in hell, but we don't hear about song, because there's no song there, there's no poetry there, there's no music there. There's plenty of it on earth, even among the unsaved persons, because they were made in the image of God. And so while they have lost God from their mind, they still appreciate the sublime. . . .

Jesus our Lord said, "God is a Spirit: and they that worship him must . . ." (John 4:24). Now I want you to see that word, that imperative there. The word *must* clears away all the obscurity and takes worship out of the hands of men. You know, man wants to worship God, but he wants to worship God the way he wants to worship God. So did Cain, and so did the Samaritans, and so have they down the years, and God rejected it all. Jesus our Lord said, "God is a Spirit: and they that worship him must" . . . and He settled forever that He's going to tell us how we should worship God. And here, as a man said, "God formed a living flame, and He gave the reasoning mind, then only He may claim the worship of mankind." Instead of our worshiping God every-man-after-his-own fashion, there's only one way to worship. "I am the way, the truth, and the life: no man cometh unto the Father, but by me" (John 14:6). So instead of being kindly and charitable by allowing an idea to stand that God accepts worship from anybody anywhere, I'm injuring, jeopardizing the future man that I allow to get away with that.

I could not possibly be a politician. I could not. When some politicians met in Chicago, they had different preachers open with prayer every day, you know. And I confess that my heart curled up in scorn when I heard these preachers pray. They were so afraid that they were going to insult a Jew or make a Hamman feel bad that they picked as carefully as though they were walking among eggs for fear that they would hurt somebody's feelings if they mentioned Jesus in their prayers. But when they got out to San Francisco in the cow barn and they asked a Presbyterian preacher to pray, that Presbyterian preacher ended with "This we ask in the name of Jesus Christ our Lord. Amen."

"God is a Spirit: and they that worship him must . . ." And these altars of Baal, these churches where they pray in the spirit of Jesus *and* in the spirit of good *and* in the name of the great father *and* in the name of brotherhood—they even pray in the name of brotherhood! Well, it's too bad. And hear now the truth. The truth Himself incarnated says, "God is spirit and we must worship him in spirit and in truth." The worshiper must submit to truth, or he can't worship God. He can write poems and he can get elevations of thought when he sees a sunrise. He can hear the fledgling lark sing when fledgling larks don't sing. He can do all sorts of things, but he can't worship God acceptably, because to do so means that he's got to submit to the truth about

God. He's got to admit that God is who He is and what He says He is, and he's got to admit that Christ is who He says He is and what He says He is. And he's got to admit the truth about himself, that he's as bad a sinner as God says he is. And he has to admit the truth of atonement, that the blood of Jesus Christ cleanses and delivers from that sin, and he has to come God's way. He must be renewed after the image of Him who created him. Only the renewed man can worship God acceptably. Only the redeemed man can worship God acceptably. . . .

He must also have had an infusion of the Spirit of truth. . . . Remember that in the Old Testament, no priest could offer a sacrifice until he had been anointed with oil. He had to be anointed with oil symbolic of the Spirit of God. No man can worship out of his own heart. Let him search among the flowers; let him search among bird's nest and tombs, wherever he chooses to worship God. He cannot worship out of his own heart. Only the Holy Ghost can worship God acceptably. And He must, in us, reflect back the glory of God. The Spirit comes down to us and reflects back the glory of God. And if it does not reach our hearts, there's no reflection back and no worship. O how big and broad and incomprehensible and wonderful the work of Christ is. That's why I can't have too much sympathy for the kind of Christianity that makes it out that the gospel is to save a fellow from smoking. Is that all Christianity is? To keep me from some bad habit? Of course, a new birth will make a man right! But the purpose of God in redemption is to restore us again to the divine imperative of worship so that we can hear God say again, "So shall the king greatly desire thy beauty: for he is thy Lord; and worship thou him" (Ps. 45:11).

6

WORSHIP HE WHO IS MAJESTIC AND MEEK

*The LORD reigns, let the earth be glad; let the
distant shores rejoice. Clouds and thick darkness
surround him; righteousness and justice
are the foundation of his throne.*

PSALM 97:1–2

It is wonderful to know that somewhere in the universe there is something sound and right. I often quote with a bit of good humor the saying of the serious-minded old man of God: "If you'd be peaceful and have peace in your heart, don't inquire into people's lives too closely. The idea is you'll be shocked if you do." But here's a throne that's filled with righteousness and judgment. "His lightnings enlightened the world: the earth saw, and trembled. The hills melted like wax at the presence of the LORD, at the presence of the Lord of the whole earth. The heavens declare his righteousness" (Ps. 97:4–5). You can search for a million years and beyond and you'll not find anything wrong there. The throne of God stands right, and the God who sits on that throne is right. He is the God of righteousness, and the heavens declare His righteousness. "And all the people see his glory. Confounded be all they that serve graven images, that boast themselves of idols: worship him, all ye gods. Zion heard, and was glad; and the daughters of Judah rejoiced because of thy judgments, O LORD. For thou, LORD, art high above all the earth: thou art exalted far above all gods" (vv. 6–9).

Now that's part of what the ninety-seventh psalm says about Him. And after man had fallen, he lost the vision of that glory. Yet the man of God, the martyr Stephen said, "The God of glory appeared unto our father Abraham" (Acts 7:2), and God began to reveal the glory that had been eclipsed.

Now you know that when a thing is eclipsed it doesn't mean that its light has diminished any, that its glory has anywise diminished. It means merely that there is something between us and that shining frame. When the sun is eclipsed, the sun is not one degree cooler than it was before. Nor does its flames flash out from its surface one inch shorter than it did before. It's still as hot and as big and as powerful and as free as it was before it went into eclipse, because it's not the sun that's eclipsed. It's us that is eclipsed! And we ought to get that straight. The sun is all right, and so is the great God Almighty. The glory of God shines bright as ever, and the God of glory began to appear to people. He appeared unto Abraham, and in the development of His redemptive purpose, He began to show what He wants.

We were in pretty bad shape. Read the first chapter of Romans if you want to know how bad we were. We'd gotten down to where we not only worshiped the man, which was bad enough; but we worshiped the beast, which was worse. Not only did we worship beasts as the human race, but we worshiped birds and fish and serpents. Crawling, slithering serpents. We worshiped them. Now if that wasn't bad enough, we worshiped bugs and beetles. We worshiped clear down as far as anything irregular or crawling. We got down on our knees and said, "Lord, my god!"

Now that's how bad our minds were in eclipse. For it was our minds and not God. Then God began to appear out from behind the cloud. The God of glory appeared to Abraham and He revealed His oneness. Now that was the first thing that God revealed about Himself. He didn't reveal His holiness first. He revealed His oneness first.

It was an insult to the great God Almighty to think that there were two or three god almighties. Did you ever stop to think that there can't be two infinites and that there can't be two omnipotents? Is it possible for two beings to be almighty? For if one being had all the power there is, then where would the second being come in? You couldn't have all the power there is. You couldn't have two beings having all the power there is.

Then we come to infinitude, which means "boundless or limitless" in its complete, absolute sense. So how could there be two beings who are absolute? There could be one, but there couldn't be two. You see, it is metaphysically impossible to even think of two beings who are absolute, who are infinite, who are almighty, who are omnipotent, or any of the other attributes of God. But we didn't know that, so we worshiped everything that would move, and if it didn't move, we got down in front of it and worshiped it anyway. We worshiped everything! We worshiped the trees, the sun, the stars, and we had gods everywhere.

It seems strange and almost humorous to you and me, but it was a long way from being humorous when the Almighty told the people, "Hear, O Israel: The LORD our God is one LORD" (Deut. 6:4). That was the oneness. Scholars call that "monotheism." That is their way of hiding the meaning from the people and giving people the impression that they are very learned. But all monotheism means is that there is one God. There is one God, and we thought there were many. The human race thought there were many. I have a book on the gods by Cicero. Cicero, the mighty man that he was, thought that there was more than one god. So God said, "Now the first thing you're going to have to get straight is that I have no rival. There is no other god by me. Hear, O Israel! Hear, O Israel, the Lord thy God is one Lord, and Him only shalt thou worship." And centuries later, a Christian sang this:

> One God ! one Majesty! There is
> no God but Thee! Unbounded,
> unextended Unity!
>
> Awful in unity,
> O God! we worship Thee,
> More simply one, because supremely Three!
>
> Dread, unbeginning One!
> Single, yet not alone,
> Creation hath not set Thee on a higher throne

Unfathomable Sea!
All life is out of Thee,
And Thy life is Thy blissful Unity.

The Christians knew this:

All things that from Thee run,
All works that Thou hast done,
Thou didst in honor of Thy being One.
Blest be Thy Unity!
All joys are one to me,—
The joy that there can be no other God than Thee!

Now this was what the Christians sang, and this is what Christians believe. This is just what Jesus taught. And little by little, God came out from behind that eclipse.

I like to go back to the Exodus if I feel I amount to anything or if I get awe struck a little by a queen or a president or somebody. I like to go back to the book of Exodus where it says, "And the LORD said unto Moses, 'Lo, I come unto thee in a thick cloud, that the people may hear when I speak with thee, and believe thee for ever'" (19:9). Moses told the people, and then the Lord said, "Go unto the people, and sanctify them to day and to morrow, and let them wash their clothes" (19:10). You didn't come rushing into that awesome presence. You had to get ready and get sanctified.

I don't know what *Life* magazine would have done about this. I supposed they would have wanted to photograph it. But "thou shalt set bounds unto the people round about, saying, Take heed to yourselves, that ye go not up into the mount, or touch the border of it: whosoever toucheth the mount shall be surely put to death" (19:12). What a contrast between this great God and the gods that they could handle and lug around and put under their pillow. "There shall not an hand touch it," He said, "but he shall surely be stoned, or shot through; whether it be beast or man, it shall not live: when the trumpet soundeth long, they shall come up to the mount" (19:13). . . .

You know what we've done? We've brought God down until nobody can respect Him anymore. I was preaching once in New York City and said, "I'm on a quiet little crusade, not as big as the one over there at Madison Square Garden, but a quiet little crusade to bring worship back to the church." And a fine looking English gentleman said to me as we were moving out of church, "Brother Tozer, I want to be a member of your crusade. For twenty-seven years I've been a missionary in the Far East. I'm home now, and I think we ought to get back to worshiping God again, that mighty and that terrible God."

The gospel has gone down now to the place where it's good only for what you can get out of it. We forget that the Lord said, "When ye pray, say, Our Father which art in heaven, Hallowed be thy name" (Luke 11:2). I don't hesitate to say that God Almighty would rather glorify His name than save a world, that God would rather His name be hallowed before all the myriads, all created intelligences and sinners be saved or a world be redeemed. In the wisdom and mercy of God, He so arranged things that He can redeem the world and magnify His own glory. But you and I have the first duty and obligation to honor God, not the duty and obligation to help people. That's modernism, and they've had that thrown on us. Our Puritan, Dutch, and Scotch forefathers who said, "Let God be right if the world falls," have been shoved aside. And they tell us that God is so very kind and lowly and humble and meek and approachable that we've taken all the meaning out of it.

Fear this glorious and fearful name, Jehovah, thy God. Shall not His excellency make you afraid? And His dread fall upon you? And with God a terrible majesty and darkness is round about Him. And His pavilion round about were dark waters and thick clouds of the sky. "Who is this King of glory? The LORD strong and mighty, the LORD mighty in battle" (Ps. 24:8). "When ye pray, say, 'Father . . . hallowed be thy name'" (Luke 11:2). And "They speak of the glorious splendor of your majesty —and I will meditate on your wonderful works" (Ps. 145:5).

I'm just giving you what the Bible says about God's coming out from behind the cloud, or His bringing us out from behind the cloud to show how great He is. "The LORD shall cause his glorious voice to be heard, and shall shew the lighting down of his arm, with the indignation of his anger, and with the flame of a devouring fire, with scattering, and tempest, and hailstones" (Isa. 30:30).

"That's the Old Testament," somebody says, "but in the New Testament, we have the meek and lowly Jesus." Well, we do, and I want to talk about the lowly and the meek Jesus, too. But I want you to know that the meek Jesus is a long way from being the Jesus of Solomon's bearded, feminine head. I don't believe in these feminine heads of Christ. I wouldn't have one in my home any more than I would have a statue of the virgin Mary. I wouldn't have one around because that's not Jesus.

That weak-looking, plaintive fellow that's looking around for somewhere to hide or for somebody to bless. "At the name of Jesus," says the Holy Ghost, "every knee should bow, of things in heaven, and things in earth, and things under the earth; and that every tongue should confess that Jesus Christ is Lord, to the glory of God the Father" (Phil. 2:10–11).

And our Lord Jesus Christ which, in His time, He shall show who is the blessed and only potentate, the King of kings and Lord of lords and only have immortality dwelling in the light which no man can approach unto and whom no man has seen or can see. To Him be honor and power everlasting, amen. That's the New Testament, brother. To the only wise God, our Savior be glory and majesty, dominion and power both now and ever, amen. That's the New Testament! And this Jesus Christ of whom we speak, He is Lord of all. He is Lord of all being and He is Lord of all life and He's the Lord of all majesty and all glory. . . .

God says, "When ye pray, say, Our Father which art in heaven, Hallowed be thy name. Thy kingdom come. Thy will be done, as in heaven, so in earth" (Luke 11:2). That's more important, my friends! It's more important that the church of Christ should honor the God of glory than they should even preach the gospel to the heathens. But it is also in the will of God that preaching the gospel to the heathen and getting them saved will, as Paul said, bring more people to praise Him. So we glorify God by winning more people. But if you had to take your choice, honoring God would be first.

I don't know who's going to do it. I talked to James Stuart of the European Missions and Stacey Woods of the InterVarsity and some of the other brethren, and we pretty much agreed. We stood around there and looked at each other and said, "Well, when's this thing going to get together and start to flow? When is there going to be enough of these people who believe in the high honor of God and the need for exalting God and bringing worship back to the world again? When is there going to be enough that we can be more than a little puddle here and a little puddle there? When can we get together and become a flowing river?" Nobody had the answer yet, but one of these days God is going to give us the answer.

And if there's anything that we've got to have in the church of Christ, it is that we should get back to the God of our fathers, back again to the holy God of Abraham, Isaac, and Jacob, not to the god of our imagination, not to the weak god whom we push around, but to the great God almighty.

God is a great God, and if I had to stop, I'd stop right there. But I'm glad to tell you also that in the forty-fifth Psalm there is not only majesty, but there is also meekness: "In thy majesty ride prosperously because of truth and meekness" (Ps. 45:4). He meeked Himself. Meekness is an adjective. Meek isn't a verb, but it ought to be a verb. It used to be, and from now on it's going to be. And He meeked Himself down. Christ Jesus, "who being in the form of God, thought it not robbery to be equal with God: But made himself of no reputation" (Phil. 2:6–7).

The only person that dare make Himself of no reputation is somebody who's sure of his reputation. He could avoid His reputation because He knew it was safe. The fellow who isn't sure of himself has to defend it all the time and run about defending his reputation. Then if he hears anybody saying anything about him that might sully his reputation, he writes a hot letter.

But He made Himself of no reputation. Why? Because He knew who He was. He knew that He was this mighty Lord God that made the mount to quake. He knew He was this mighty Lord God whose pavilions round about Him were dark water and thick cloud in the sky. He knew He was the King of glory and Lord of majesty. Blessed be His glorious name forever. He wasn't afraid to void His reputation for the sake of redeeming a lost world. So He made Himself of no reputation.

Now that's one thing, but it's another thing to take on Himself the form of a man—the form of a servant first, really. That's something. The great God who had given orders all His life and had lived before the world was and who had being before creation was—now He became a servant. Not only did He take no reputation, but He became a servant and was made in the likeness of men.

And after He'd become a man, He humbled Himself still further and became obedient unto death. But that was not low enough, so He died even the death of the cross. If He had come down from glory and had lived His life and had gotten old and died in His bed surrounded by weeping friends, it would have been terrible to think that the great Lord God Almighty whose strength and beauty were in His sanctuary should die. But He died in the worst form known at the time. He died on a Roman cross. Sweating, and His bones pulled out of joint, and His lips cracked, and His eyes glazed—He died like that. "Even," says the Holy Ghost, "death of the cross." What wondrous condescension that He should be so meek.

If you ever get saved, if you ever move into that heaven of God and walk through those holy gates and look upon the silvery sea, it will not be because of anything you are. And it won't be because He changed His mind or because He lost His crown or His power. . . . Brethren, nobody has ever trimmed down the majesty of the great God Almighty. And when Jesus Christ became a man, He didn't lose anything. The theologian Lightfoot said, "He veiled His glory, but He did not void it!"

The man who walked about in Jerusalem with dust covered feet and disheveled hair, walking in the wind from one place to another, was the same Lord God who could make the mighty come down with His voice. This is our Christ. This is our Jesus. And I recommend to you, my friend, that you seek to know Him as He is in His majesty in order that you might know how mighty fortunate you are. If He had stood by His majesty and had not been willing to meek Himself down, you'd have been in bad shape. You'd have been along with the angels that sinned and left their first habitation. You'd have gone down. And there wasn't anything in you that could save you. When you started down toward the pit the day you took your first step or before, not an angelic voice said, "God, what are you doing? Don't let that fellow perish. Don't let that woman die." Not a one where justice and majesty and glory were demanded. We all perish together and go to hell where the devil and the fallen angels are. And to save us from that, God would not have voided His majesty. Keep that in mind. To save us from that, God would not have diminished His glory. To save us from that, God would have never have unhallowed His hallowed name.

When the great God Almighty meeked Himself, when such majesty meeked itself downward, "so shall the king greatly desire thy beauty" (Ps. 45:11). Why did He do it? Because He greatly desired thy beauty. And the beauty in you is not the beauty you have, but the beauty that He could put in you.

It was what Shakespeare called the "borrowed majesty." The borrowed majesty that belonged to you and even the poor tramp who stumbles, blear-eyed and unshaven on skid row, has within him buried some of the borrowed majesty, for God made us in His own image. That doesn't save us, but there was something there that God called beautiful. And so He came down. And He didn't come down because He had to. Never think you can put God in a tight spot. God never gets into tight spots, and God never allows Himself to be taken over by a man, put into a tight corner, and forced to do something that He doesn't want to do. The great God came down because He desired us, and He desired us because He made us in His image. That's all. He made us in His image. He saw the poor, tattered relics of a family resemblance. And He knew there was that in us which could respond. He knew that though fallen and lost and certainly doomed, there was that in us which could respond.

For that you ought to thank God every day you live. If anybody here grumbles and complains and doesn't keep thanking. God, I'm sorry for you and I hope you'll repent. For no matter what happens to us, we ought to be able to thank God that there was something in us that could respond. Aren't you glad that there was something in us that could respond?

I'm not even sure that if God hadn't put it there in the first place that we could have responded at all. Because if I understand the book of John and the book of Romans correctly, I don't believe that there is anything in mankind that can respond except that it is first moved upon by the Holy Ghost. I believe in the prevenient workings of the Holy Ghost. If that isn't election and predestination, I don't know what is, but it must be. Although I'm not supposed to teach either. But Jesus, who is my Lord, said that, "No man can come to me except the Father draw him." No man can come, and we say, "Come on! Come on! Come on!" And He said, "No man can come except the Father draw him." And if the Father draw him, he'll come. "I'll give him life and won't cast him out." He said, "You believe not because you are not my sheep." He didn't say, "You're not my sheep because you don't believe."

We turn it around because we're afraid to face up to the sovereign majesty of the God of our fathers. And so we say, "The reason you're not God's sheep is because you don't believe." But He said, "The reason you don't believe is because you're not my sheep! I have not chosen you."

Now I realize that there has been an awful lot of abuse. As the queen said, "Oh, Liberty, what sins have been committed in thy name." We can only say, "John Calvin, what crimes have been committed in thy name." But nevertheless, my brethren, we're a snooty bunch of self-satisfied sinners. We think that when we get good and ready, and whatever God thinks of it, we'll come back home, and God will receive us, and He can't help Himself. We had better get away from that.

We so preach the gospel as to make grace cheap and God cheap and make God owe us something. What does God owe us except damnation? What does he owe the old Archbishop of Canterbury or the Pope except damnation? We have sinned! And we have veiled the glory of God and we've taken our place with the fallen crew and black bats and the squirming serpents, and if we're ever saved it is because majesty meeked itself down to find us. And majesty didn't have to do it because majesty wasn't afraid of itself. We rush to defend God. I wouldn't write one line in defense of God. When Gideon pulled the alters down somebody said, "Kill Gideon! He's pulled down the alters of Baal." And Gideon's father said, "If Baal's a god, why doesn't he look after himself?" He said, "You have to run out there and defend him? Let Baal plead. And if Baal is what he claims he is, let him punish my son. I'm not going to defend him."

A god I have to defend can't take me across the dark river. He can't save my soul from the magnetic tug of hell. A god I have to defend can't deliver me from the devil. Oh, my God doesn't need my defense. He's the Lord of glory. Mighty and great is He. And He meeked Himself down.

He became meek because He was majesty. You deserve nothing but death, but He died that you might be called to Him. What a wonderful, gracious God He is.

AWED BY GOD'S PRESENCE

"Woe to me!" I cried. "I am ruined! For I am a man
of unclean lips, and I live among a people of unclean lips,
and my eyes have seen the King, the LORD Almighty."

ISAIAH 6:5

Through the years, I have quite often heard educated and intelligent persons say, "Let me tell you how I discovered God." Whether these discoverers went on from there to a humble and adoring worship of God I cannot say. I do know, however, that all of us would be in great trouble and still far from God if He had not graciously and in love revealed Himself to us.

I am a little irritated or grieved at the continuing hope of so many people that they will be able to grasp God—understand God, commune with God—through their intellectual capacities. When will they realize that if they could possibly "discover" God with the intellect, they would be equal to God?

We would do well to lean toward the kind of discovery of God described by the prophet Isaiah: "In the year that king Uzziah died I saw also the Lord sitting upon a throne, high and lifted up, and his train filled the temple" (6:1). Now, that which Isaiah saw was wholly other than, and altogether different from, anything he had ever seen before. Up to this point in his life, Isaiah had become familiar with the good things God had created. But he had never been introduced to the presence of the Uncreated. To Isaiah, then, the violent contrast between that which is God and that which is not God was such that his very language suffered under the effort to express it. Significantly, God was revealing Himself to man. Isaiah could have tried for a million years to reach God by means of his intellect without any chance of succeeding. All of the accumulated brainpower in the whole world could not reach God. But the living God, in the space of a short second of time, can reveal Himself to the willing spirit of a man. It is only then that an Isaiah, or any other man or woman, can say with humility but with assurance, "I know Him."

Unlike men, God never acts without purpose. Here God was revealing Himself to Isaiah for eternal purposes. Isaiah has tried to give us a true record, but what actually happened is greater than what Isaiah wrote by as much as God is greater than the human mind. Isaiah confesses that he had never before seen the Lord sitting upon a throne. Modern critics of this record by Isaiah warn us of the danger of anthropomorphism—the attempt to bestow upon God certain human attributes.

I have never been afraid of big words. Let them call it what they will, I still believe that God sits upon a throne, invested with self-bestowed sovereignty. I believe, too, that God sits upon a throne determining all events, finally, according to the purpose which He purposed in Christ Jesus before the world began. Now, because we are dealing with worship, let us consider the joys and delights of the heavenly creatures, the seraphim, around the throne of God. This is Isaiah's record:

> Above it stood the seraphims: each one had six wings; with twain he covered his face, and with twain he covered his feet, and with twain he did fly.
> And one cried unto another, and said, Holy, holy, holy, is the LORD of hosts: the whole earth is full of his glory. (6:2–3)

We know very little about these created beings, but I am impressed by their attitude of exalted worship. They are close to the throne and they burn with rapturous love for the Godhead. They were engrossed in their antiphonal chants, "Holy, holy, holy!"

I have often wondered why the rabbis and saints and hymnists of those olden times did not come to the knowledge of the Trinity just from the seraphims' praise, "Holy, holy, holy." I am a Trinitarian—I believe in one God, the Father Almighty, maker of heaven and earth. I believe in one Lord Jesus Christ, Son of the Father, begotten of Him before all ages. I believe in the Holy Spirit, the Lord and giver of life, who with the Father and Son together is worshiped and glorified. This is a very moving scene—the seraphim worshiping God. The more I read my Bible the more I believe in the triune God.

In Isaiah's vision the seraphim were chanting their praises to the Trinity 800 years before Mary cried with joy and her Baby wailed in Bethlehem's manger, when the second person of the

Trinity, the eternal Son, came to earth to dwell among us. The key words then and the keynote still of our worship must be "Holy, holy, holy!"

I am finding that many Christians are really not comfortable with the holy attributes of God. In such cases I am forced to wonder about the quality of the worship they try to offer to Him. The word "holy" is more than an adjective saying that God is a holy God—it is an ecstatic ascription of glory to the triune God. I am not sure that we really know what it means, but I think we should attempt a definition.

Complete moral purity can only describe God. Everything that appears to be good among men and women must be discounted, for we are human. Not one of us is morally pure. Abraham, David and Elijah; Moses, Peter and Paul—all were good men. They were included in God's fellowship. But each had his human flaws and weaknesses as members of Adam's race. Each had to find the place of humble repentance. Because God knows our hearts and our intentions, He is able to restore His sincere and believing children who are in the faith.

Much of our problem in continuing fellowship with a holy God is that many Christians repent only for what they do, rather than for what they are. It should help us to be concerned about the quality of our worship when we consider that Isaiah's reaction was a feeling of absolute profaneness in the presence of the moral purity of the divine Being. Consider that Isaiah was a commendable young man—cultured, religious, and a cousin of the king. He would have made a good deacon in any church. Today he would be asked to serve on one of our mission boards.

But here Isaiah was an astonished man. He was struck with

awe, his whole world suddenly dissolving into a vast, eternal brightness. He was pinned against that brightness—red and black, the colors of sin. What had happened? Isaiah, only human, had glimpsed One whose character and nature signaled perfection. He could only manage the witness: "Mine eyes have seen the King" (Isa. 6:5).

The definition of "Holy, holy" must certainly have room for "mystery" if, in our attempts to worship, we are to have an effective appreciation of our God. There are leaders in various Christian circles who know so much about the things of God that they will offer to answer every question you may have. We can hope to answer questions helpfully as far as we can. But there is a sense of divine mystery running throughout all of the kingdom of God—far beyond the mystery that scientists discover running throughout the kingdom of nature.

There are those who pretend to know everything about God—who pretend they can explain everything about God, about His creation, about His thoughts and about His judgments. They have joined the ranks of the evangelical rationalists. They end up taking the mystery out of life and the mystery out of worship. When they have done that, they have taken God out as well. The kind of "know-it-all" attitude about God that we see in some teachers today leaves them in a very difficult position. They must roundly criticize and condemn any other man taking any position slightly different from theirs. Our cleverness and glibness and fluency may well betray our lack of that divine awe upon our spirits, silent and wonderful, that breathes a whisper, "Oh, Lord God, Thou knowest."

In Isaiah 6 we see a clear portrayal of what happens to a

person in the mystery of the presence. Isaiah, overpowered within his own being, can only confess humbly, "I am a man of unclean lips." I remind you that Isaiah recognized the "strangeness"—something of the mystery of the person of God. In that presence, Isaiah found no place for joking or for clever cynicism or for human familiarity. He found a strangeness in God, that is, a presence unknown to the sinful and worldly and self-sufficient human. A person who has sensed what Isaiah sensed will never be able to joke about "the Man upstairs" or the "Someone up there who likes me." One of the movie actresses who still prowled around the nightclubs after her supposed conversion to Christ was quoted as telling someone, "You ought to know God. You know, God is just a livin' doll!" I read where another man said, "God is a good fellow."

I confess that when I hear or read these things I feel a great pain within. My brother or sister, there is something about our God that is *different*, that is beyond us, that is above us—transcendent. We must be humbly willing to throw our hearts open and to plead, "God, shine Thyself into my understanding for I will never find Thee otherwise." The mystery, the strangeness is in God. Our Lord does not expect us to behave like zombies when we become Christians. But He does expect that we will have our soul open to the mystery that is God. I think it is proper for us to say that a genuine Christian should be a walking mystery because he surely is a walking miracle. Through the leading and the power of the Holy Spirit, the Christian is involved in a daily life and habit that cannot be explained. A Christian should have upon him an element that is beyond psychology—beyond all natural laws and into spiritual laws.

God is a consuming fire. We are told that it is a fearful thing to fall into the hands of the living God. Do you recall the first chapter of Ezekiel? The dejected prophet saw heaven opened. He was given a vision of God. And he then witnessed four-faced creatures out of the fire.

I think in our witness and ministries, we Christians should be men and women out of the fire. Because our God is holy, He is actively hostile to sin. God can only burn on and on against sin forever. In another passage Isaiah asked, "Who among us shall dwell with the devouring fire? who among us shall dwell with everlasting burnings?" (Isa. 33:14).

Isaiah was not thinking about those who would be separated from God. He was thinking of a company who would live for God and dwell with God. He answers his own question: "He that walketh righteously, and speaketh uprightly; . . . he shall dwell on high" (Isa. 33:15–16).

The Salvation Army has always had as its slogan "Blood and Fire." I am for that in the things of God. We know of cleansing by the blood of Christ. The references to God's workings often have to do with a holy flame. John the Baptist pointed to Christ's coming and said, "I indeed baptize you with water unto repentance: . . . he shall baptize you with the Holy Ghost, and with fire" (Matt. 3:11).

When Isaiah cried out, "I am undone!" it was a cry of pain. It was the revealing cry of conscious uncleanness. He was experiencing the undoneness of the creature set over against the holiness of the Creator.

What should happen in genuine conversion? What should a man or woman feel in the transaction of the new birth? There ought to be that real and genuine cry of pain. That is why I do not like the kind of evangelism that tries to invite people into the fellowship of God by signing a card. There should be a birth from above and within. There should be the terror of seeing ourselves in violent contrast to the holy, holy, holy God. Unless we come into this place of conviction and pain, I am not sure how deep and real our repentance will ever be.

Today, it is not a question of whether we have Isaiah's cleanness, but a question of whether we have his awareness. He was unclean and, thank God, he became aware of it. But the world today is unclean and seems to be almost totally unaware of it. Uncleanness with unawareness will have terrible consequences. That is what is wrong with the Christian church and with our Protestantism. Our problem is the depravity still found within the circle of the just, among those called to be saints, among those who claim to be great souls.

We like Isaiah's vision and awareness. But we do not like to think of the live coal out of the fire being placed on the prophet's lips in purification by blood and by fire. Isaiah's lips, symbolic of all his nature, were purified by fire. God could then say to him, "Thine iniquity is taken away" (Isa. 6:7). That is how the amazed and pained Isaiah could genuinely come to a sense of restored moral innocence. That is how he instantly found that he was ready for worship and that he was also ready and anxious for service in the will of God. With each of us, if we are to have that assurance of forgiveness and restored moral innocence, the fire of God's grace must touch us. It is only through the depths of the forgiving love of God that men and women can be so restored and made ready to serve Him.

In the same vein, is there any other way in which we, the creatures of God, can become prepared and ready to worship Him? I can only remind you of our great needs in this terrible day when men and women are trying their best to cut God down to their size. Many also believe that it is possible to gain control of the sovereign God and to think Him down to a plane where they can use Him as they want to. Even in our Christian circles we are prone to depend upon techniques and methods in the work that Christ has given us to do. Without a complete dependence upon the Holy Spirit we can only fail. If we have been misled to believe that we can do Christ's work ourselves, it will never be done. The man whom God will use must be undone. He must be a man who has seen the King in His beauty. Let us never take anything for granted about ourselves, my brother or sister.

Do you know who gives me the most trouble? Do you know who I pray for the most in my pastoral work? Just myself. I do not say it to appear to be humble, for I have preached all my lifetime to people who are better than I. I tell you again that God has saved us to be worshipers. May God show us a vision of ourselves that will disvalue us to the point of total devaluation. From there He can raise us up to worship Him and to praise Him and to witness.

8

GENUINE WORSHIP INVOLVES FEELING

But I trust in your unfailing love; my heart rejoices
in your salvation. I will sing the LORD's praise,
for he has been good to me.

PSALM 13:5–6

How long do you think it will be, if Jesus tarries, before some of the amazing new churches like those in the primitive Baliem Valley of Irian Jaya, Indonesia, will be sending gospel missionaries to Canada and the United States? If that thought upsets you, you desperately need to read this chapter.

I have a reason for suggesting this as a possibility at some time in the future. In Chicago, I was introduced to a deeply serious Christian brother who had come from his native India with a stirring and grateful testimony of the grace of God in his life. I asked him about his church background, of course. He was not Pentecostal. He was neither Anglican nor Baptist. He was neither Presbyterian nor Methodist. He did not even know what we mean by the label, "interdenominational." He was simply a brother in Christ. This Indian had been born into the Hindu religion, but he was converted to and became a disciple of Jesus Christ by reading and seriously studying the New Testament record of the death and resurrection of our Lord. He spoke English well enough to express his Christian concerns for the world and for the churches. I asked him to speak in my pulpit.

Through that encounter I realized that unless we arouse ourselves spiritually, unless we are brought back to genuine love and adoration and worship, our candlestick could be removed. We may need missionaries coming to us, indeed. We may need them to show us what genuine and vital Christianity is! We should never forget that God created us to be joyful worshipers, but sin drew us into everything else but worship. Then in God's love and mercy in Christ Jesus, we were restored into the fellowship of the Godhead through the miracle of the new birth.

"You have been forgiven and restored," God reminds us. "I am your Creator and Redeemer and Lord, and I delight in your worship."

I don't know, my friend, how that makes you feel—but I feel that I must give God the full response of my heart. I am happy to be counted as a worshiper.

Well, that word "feel" has crept in here, and I know that you may have an instant reaction against it. In fact, I have had people tell me very dogmatically that they will never allow "feeling" to have any part in their spiritual life and experience. I reply, "Too bad for you!" I say that because I have voiced a very real definition of what I believe true worship to be: worship is to feel in the heart! In the Christian faith, we should be able to use the word *feel* boldly and without apology. What worse thing could be said of us as the Christian church if it could be said that we are a feelingless people?

Worship must always come from an inward attitude. It embodies a number of factors, including the mental, spiritual and emotional. You may not at times worship with the same degree of wonder and love that you do at other times, but the attitude and the state of mind are consistent if you are worshiping the Lord.

A husband and father may not appear to love and cherish his family with the same intensity when he is discouraged, when he is tired from long hours in business or when events have made him feel depressed. He may not outwardly show as much love toward his family, but it is there, nonetheless, for it is not a feeling only. It is an attitude and a state of mind. It is a sustained act, subject to varying degrees of intensity and perfection.

I came into the kingdom of God with joy, knowing that I had been forgiven. I do know something of the emotional life that goes along with conversion to Christ. I well remember, however, that in my early Christian fellowship, there were those who warned me about the dangers of "feeling." They cited the biblical example of Isaac feeling the arms of Jacob and thinking they were Esau's. Thus the man who went by his feelings was mistaken! That sounds interesting, but it is not something on which you can build Christian doctrine.

Think of that sick woman in the gospel record who had had an issue of blood for twelve years and had suffered many things of many physicians. Mark records that when she had heard of Jesus, she came in the throng and merely touched His garment. In the same instant "the fountain of her blood was dried up; and she felt in her body that she was healed of that plague" (Mark 5:29). Knowing what had been done within her by the Savior, she "came and fell down before him, and told him all the truth" (5:33). Her testimony was in worship and praise. She felt in her body that she was healed.

Those of us who have been blessed within our own beings would not join in any crusade to "follow your feelings." On the other hand, if there is no feeling at all in our hearts, then we are dead! If you wake up tomorrow morning and there is absolute numbness in your right arm—no feeling at all—you will quickly dial the doctor with your good left hand.

Real worship is, among other things, a feeling about the Lord our God. It is in our hearts. And we must be willing to express it in an appropriate manner. We can express our worship to God in many ways. But if we love the Lord and are led by His Holy Spirit, our worship will always bring a delighted sense of admiring awe and a sincere humility on our part.

The proud and lofty man or woman cannot worship God any more acceptably than can the proud devil himself. There must be humility in the heart of the person who would worship God in spirit and in truth.

The manner in which many moderns think about worship makes me uncomfortable. Can true worship be engineered and manipulated? Do you foresee with me the time to come when churches may call the pastor a "spiritual engineer"? I have heard of psychiatrists being called "human engineers," and of course, they are concerned with our heads. We have reduced so many things to engineering or scientific or psychological terms that the coming of "spiritual engineers" is a possibility. But this will never replace what I have called the astonished wonder wherever worshipers are described in the Bible.

We find much of spiritual astonishment and wonder in the book of Acts. You will always find these elements present when the Holy Spirit directs believing men and women. On the other hand, you will not find astonished wonder among men and women when the Holy Spirit is not present.

Engineers can do many great things in their fields, but no mere human force or direction can work the mysteries of God among men. If there is no wonder, no experience of mystery, our efforts to worship will be futile. There will be no worship without the Spirit. If God can be understood and comprehended by any of our human means, then I cannot worship Him. One thing is sure. I will never bend my knees and say "Holy, holy, holy" to that which I have been able to decipher and figure out in my own mind! That which I can explain will never bring me to the place of awe. It can never fill me with astonishment or wonder or admiration.

The philosophers called the ancient mystery of the personhood of God the "*mysterium conundrum.*" We who are God's children by faith call Him "our Father which art in heaven." In sections of the church where there is life and blessing and wonder in worship, there is also the sense of divine mystery. Paul epitomized it for us as "Christ in you, the hope of glory" (Col.1:27).

What does happen, then, in a Christian church when a fresh and vital working of the Spirit of God brings revival? In my study and observations, a revival generally results in a sudden bestowment of a spirit of worship. This is not the result of engineering or of manipulation. It is something God bestows on people hungering and thirsting for Him. With spiritual renewing will come a blessed spirit of loving worship. These believers worship gladly because they have a high view of God. In some circles, God has been abridged, reduced, modified, edited, changed and amended until He is no longer the God whom Isaiah saw, high and lifted up. Because He has been reduced in the minds of so many people, we no longer have that boundless confidence in His character that we used to have. He is the God to whom we go without doubts, without fears. We know He will not deceive us or cheat us. He will not break His covenant or change His mind. We have to be convinced so we can go into His presence in absolute confidence. In our hearts is this commitment: "Let God be true, but every man a liar" (Rom. 3:4). The God of the whole earth cannot do wrong! He does not need to be rescued. It is man's inadequate concept of God that needs to be rescued. Thankfully, when God made us in His own image, He gave us the capability to appreciate and admire His attributes.

I once heard Dr. George D. Watson, one of the great Bible teachers of his generation, point out that men can have two kinds of love for God—the love of gratitude or the love of excellence. He urged that we go on from gratefulness to a love of God just because He is God and because of the excellence of His character. Unfortunately, God's children rarely go beyond the boundaries of gratitude. I seldom hear anyone in worshipful prayer admiring and praising God for His eternal excellence.

Many of us are strictly "Santa Claus" Christians. We think of God as putting up the Christmas tree and putting our gifts underneath. That is only an elementary kind of love. We need to go on. We need to know the blessing of worshiping in the presence of God without thought of wanting to rush out again. We need to be delighted in the presence of utter, infinite excellence. Such worship will have the ingredient of fascination, of high moral excitement. Plainly, some of the men and women in the Bible knew this kind of fascination in their fellowship with God. If Jesus the Son is to be known and loved and served, the Holy Spirit must be allowed to illuminate our human lives. That personality will then be captured and entranced by the presence of God.

What is it that makes a human cry out:

"O Jesus, Jesus, dearest Lord!
Forgive me if I say,
For very love, Thy sacred name
A thousand times a day.

"Burn, burn, O love, within my heart,
Burn fiercely night and day,
Till all the dross of earthly loves
Is burned, and burned away."

Those expressions came from the worshiping heart of Frederick Faber. He was completely fascinated by all he had experienced in the presence and fellowship of a loving God and Savior. He was surely filled with an intensity of moral excitement. He was struck with wonder at the inconceivable magnitude and moral splendor of the Being whom we call our God. Such fascination with God must necessarily have an element of adoration. You may ask me for a definition of adoration in this context. I will say that when we adore God, all of the beautiful ingredients of worship are brought to white, incandescent heat with the fire of the Holy Spirit. To adore God means we love Him with all the powers within us. We love Him with fear and wonder and yearning and awe.

The admonition to "love the Lord thy God with all thy heart, . . . and with all thy mind" (Matt. 22:37) can mean only one thing. It means to adore Him. I use the word "adore" sparingly, for it is a precious word. I love babies, and I love people, but I cannot say I adore them. Adoration I keep for the only One who deserves it. In no other presence and before no other being can I kneel in reverent fear and wonder and yearning and feel the sense of possessiveness that cries, "Mine, mine!"

They can change the expressions in the hymnals, but whenever men and women are lost in worship they will cry out, "Oh God, thou art my God; early will I seek thee" (Ps. 63:1). Worship becomes a completely personal love experience between God and the worshiper. It was like that with David, with Isaiah, with Paul. It is like that with all whose desire has been to possess God. This is the glad truth: God is my God. Brother or sister, until you can say God and I, you cannot say "us" with any meaning. Until you have been able to meet God in loneliness of soul, just you and God—as if there was no one else in the world—you will never know what it is to love the other persons in the world.

In Canada, those who have written of the saintly Holy Anne said, "She talks to God as if there was nobody else but God and He had no other children but her." That was not a selfish quality. She had found the value and delight of pouring her personal devotion and adoration at God's feet.

Consecration is not difficult for the person who has met God.

Where there is genuine adoration and fascination, God's child wants nothing more than the opportunity to pour out his or her love at the Savior's feet.

A young man talked to me about his spiritual life. He had been a Christian for several years, but he was concerned that he might not be fulfilling the will of God for his life. He spoke of coldness of heart and lack of spiritual power. I could tell that he was discouraged—and afraid of hardness of heart. I gave him a helpful expression which has come from the writings of Bernard of Clairvaux: "My brother, only the heart is hard that does not know it is hard. Only he is hardened who does not know he is hardened. When we are concerned for our coldness, it is because of the yearning God has put there. God has not rejected us."

God puts the yearning and desire in our hearts, and He does not turn away and thus mock us. God asks us to seek His face in repentance and love, and we then find all of His gracious fullness awaiting. In God's grace, that is a promise for the whole wide world. . . . What we need among us is a genuine visitation of the Spirit. We need a sudden bestowment of the spirit of worship among God's people.

9

WORSHIP LIKE THE SERAPHIM

In the year that King Uzziah died, I saw the Lord, high and exalted, seated on a throne; and the train of his robe filled the temple. Above him were seraphim, each with six wings: With two wings they covered their faces, with two they covered their feet, and with two they were flying. And they were calling to one another: "Holy, holy, holy is the LORD Almighty; the whole earth is full of his glory."

ISAIAH 6:1–3

I n this chapter, we look through an open window into another world than the world we inhabit. We have become so used to this homey, plain, work-a-day world that we forget, or are likely to forget, that there is another world impinging upon this one—a world that is as real, or more real, more lasting than this world. And in this chapter and in a few other places in the Bible, we look in on that world, and we are forced to see and acknowledge that that world does exist.

Now of all the calamities that have ever been visited upon the world, without any doubt the surrender of the human spirit to this [eternal] world and its ways is the worst—the tyranny of material things, temporal things, things that are and then cease to be. No monarch ever ruled his cowering subjects with any more cruel tyranny than the visible things, audible things, tangible things that rule mankind. This, I say, is the worst calamity of all. . . .

Now the reality of that other world comes sometimes. I believe this. I keep repeating it because I think that in doing so, I am not only telling the truth, but I am getting very close to you, or very close to my hearers, wherever they might be. The reality of this invisible world that is near to our world and real, this world of spirits, this world of God and angels and seraphim and cherubim—the reality of this world comes to us sometimes— even in the midst of all of our modern noise and confusion. We still have times when, alone, we feel the other world. We sense it. We know that it exists. Maybe it's only for a moment that we have such a feeling—only for a little time that it comes to us. But those times do come! Man was made in the image of God and is a fallen star, a fallen being, that has left his place in the celestial world and has plummeted down like a falling star and is here in the world, and he's all but forgotten the place from which he came. But that reality does come in upon us occasionally. . . .

But the devil sees to it that we seldom get alone. When a man really gets alone, he senses sometimes that this isn't it. He looks around at everything, but this isn't it. He says to himself, *Now, I like it, and it's all right, and it has its points. There are many arguments in favor of it, but there's something in me that's telling me that this isn't it. It just isn't it. There's something else.*

We stand at the grave of some loved one to whom we've just said a tearful goodbye, and we know that this isn't it. We know that there is some other world than the one we see. We see, for a moment, the invisible. And the reality of that world breaks in upon us. Most people deal with it by abruptly breaking it off and refusing to think about it at all. But one of these times, the reality of the other world will be brought vividly present before every one of us. There will be a time when the terrifyingly sudden breaking off will take place. And then, whether we're right or whether we're wrong, whether we're in or whether we're out of the kingdom, we'll know with a knowledge that's not faith anymore, but with a knowledge that is reality—visible, tangible, audible. We'll know that there is another world beside the world in which we live.

The Christian is one who has dedicated himself to God, to inhabit another world. And that's why we get called the names we get called. We get called "psalm singers," but I don't know anything nicer than to be called a psalm singer! I know the psalms. Now if I could just sing, I would be all set and I would most happily go down the street and have men whisper behind their hand and say, "Look at that old bald-headed psalm singer going there." I think that would be a lovely thing. I can't think of anything better than to be called a psalm singer.

I picked up a book the other day, I forget what it's called, one of those infinite numbers of anthologies of poetry that are bought. This one was compiled by two of the Roosevelts, that is two of the Theodore Roosevelt family. And I sat there and leafed them over—partly read poems, some I remembered and some I hadn't seen before—and they were stirring. They were good and they were about this and that and this and that, and I read a while and thought, *You know, he's good. This poet is good. That's well said. That's good. That's well said.*

And then I lay it down and picked up the old hymn book and I began to read the hymns. Hymns of Watson and Montgomery and Wesley and the rest of them, and I said, "Oh, brother, they didn't have it. These other fellas here in the first little anthology, they were good all right, but they didn't have it. This is it."

When Wesley opens his mouth and condenses a verse of Scripture into four rhyming lines, that's it! When Isaac Watts sits down and opens heaven and shows us in a half dozen lines God and the angels and the Holy Ghost and redemption and the blood of the Lamb and salvation, that's it, brother! And I say to myself, *These others, they're just tinkerers. They hang around the edges. They're simply butterflies.* But the writers of the psalms and the writers of the hymns, they had it. They were in touch with another world. They were geared in the solid, lasting world that is the kingdom.

Now Isaiah saw that world and he said that it was the year that King Uzziah had died that he had this vision. He wrote this, I suppose, many years later, but he remembered it by the fact that it was the year that King Uzziah died. . . .

Let's consider the worship of these seraphim—these strange, six-winged creatures. Now I don't know why they had wings. I don't know why they needed six wings exactly. There are so many things I don't know. The older I get, the less I know. But the older I get, the more certainly I know the two things that I do know. That's what's so wonderful. You don't know many things, but you know some things terrifically. And so I know that there are seraphim and I know there's another world, and I know it's the world of spirits, it's the world of our God and His Son and of the Holy Ghost, and it's the world in which Christians are born when they're born again. And let the dispensationalists and the pickers of theological lint fight over this all they want. I'm happy to say that, to me, the kingdom of God is the spiritual realm ruled over by God the King into which people are born by the new birth.

You can split it all up and divide it and subdivide it and tack on a Greek verb, and when you're all through, I'll still believe what I believe—that the kingdom of God is the realm of the Holy Ghost into which men are born when they're born again.

Now these creatures, they worship God with their presence. They were there. . . . They were there and they could have been somewhere else, but they were worshiping God, as we find them here. And brethren, you worship God by being where God is.

Now there are some individualists who [believe they] have all the strength. They're little, the strength of individualists, but they say, "I don't go to church. I don't think it's necessary. I don't mingle with the people of God. I don't think it's necessary at all. I think we should retreat, and I find that just walking around on Sunday morning is enough."

Now the seraphim could have said something like that, but they didn't. They went where there was worship. And they worshiped God with their presence. Now we even have people hanging around the borders of our churches who say, "If you don't feel like going to church, don't go! If you don't feel like going to prayer meeting, don't go!" And they're perfectly free to say that if they want, but they're still down here in the flesh! And their freedom is not the pure freedom of spirits before the throne. It is the carnal license of half-converted men. Wherever God is, there you want to be. And where the people of God are, there you want to be. So the real Christian worships God with his interests and he worships God with his presence and he is there.

Then I notice they worship God with their *service*. They had feet and wings and hands, and they gave over their feet and their wings and their hands to God. And God had them all. They didn't serve God at their convenience, but a lot of people do. They were serving God freely and they didn't have to do it. But they only had three things, really: they had their feet, their wings, and their hands, and these they gave to God joyously. And they said, "Take my feet and use them at the impulse of Thy love. Take my hands, take my feet, take my silver, take my gold. Take everything." So God had everything.

You know, brother, if God gets your feet and your hands and your wings, He's just about got you. Because your feet determine where you go, and your hands determine what you do, and your wings—well, I don't know about that. I didn't take that course, so I don't know what that signifies. But if you study typology in school and you get the course, you know what that means. But if God can get your feet, brother, you won't go in the wrong places, that's all. And if God can get your hands, you won't do the wrong things.

I sat last week with Dr. Harold Lundquist and brother Phil Luo, and we were having our picture taken down at Moody Bible Institute, and we were sitting down and we had the big man in the middle and we two average-sized fellas sat around the edge. And I looked down and I said, "Brother Lundquist, that's the biggest pile of leather I've ever saw in one place in all my life."

And brother, it was. Three pairs of feet. And brother Lundquist's must be fourteens, mine are tens and a half, and brother Luo's were—they weren't exactly lady shoes, either. Well, I believe that God has the feet. God has those three pairs of feet, brother. Now they were big and they certainly weren't very handsome, but I believe that God had those three pairs of feet. And if God can get to your feet, then you're going the right place. And if He can get your hands, you're doing the right things!

But you say, "What's that got to do with worship?" Why, you worship God by where you go and what you do, not only by what you sing and by what you pray. Worship is more than prayer; worship contains prayer. Worship is more than singing; worship contains singing. But worship is also living. And in our Bible, we find worship not only to be singing, but doing and living and walking and working and going and serving, so that we can worship God with our feet by going the right way. We can worship God with our hands by doing the right thing. And if we have wings, we can worship God by flying in the right direction.

Now they had voices also here, and they *testified* their adoration. They said, "Holy, holy, holy, is the LORD of hosts: the whole earth is full of his glory" (Isa. 6:3). And it's my opinion, brethren, that the silent Christian has something wrong with him. You know that there is an abnormal psychology, called "manic depression," where people go into silence. They just shut up, and that's all. You don't talk; you just get quiet. And there they are. They grow in on themselves and keep still in on themselves, and if there's something wrong, they don't want to talk. God put a mouth on them, out there in the front of you, and He didn't mean for it to be open night and day as some people seem to imagine. But He did mean that you are to use that mouth to express some of the wonders He has generated inside your heart.

And when we come to God in Christ and we give ourselves to Him, one of the first things we do is say, "Abba, Father." I've heard it said that there are silent Christians and hidden Christians and secret Christians, and I've heard men say that we'll be surprised when we get to heaven because we'll find people there who were secret Christians who never talked about it. . . .

Oh, how foolish can we get? The things that are closest to our hearts are the things we talk about! My wife talks about her grandchildren, and you talk about that which is closest to your heart. And if it's close to your heart, you will talk about it!

Some of these old dodgers that sit around the canasta table and smoke cigarettes by the yard never bring up religion. And "if anybody says, "Well, we ought to talk about it!" And then another says there are just some things that are too sacred to mention. "I bid two spades!" says another. Well, I've never played canasta, but they excuse themselves on the grounds that there are some things too sacred to talk about. There are some things they've never seen and can't describe, and that's their trouble. There are some places they've never been, and they're not familiar with it. That's their trouble. All this quiet religion that says, "I haven't anything to say. I worship God in my heart." No, you don't.

These seraphim, they said with their voices, "Holy, holy, holy," and the Bible links faith to expression, so a faith that never gets expressed is not biblical faith. What we believe in our heart and utter forth with our lips is that Jesus Christ is Lord, and we shall be saved. . . .

God had the voices of these seraphim. I don't know what they sounded like. I should suppose they had musical voices, being seraphim. Has God got your voice? Now I ask you, has God got your voice in school? Can God make you testify? Is there something in you, an impulse that makes you want to talk about Him? Or do you discretely keep your mouth shut and say nothing? You know all about the world's ways, but when it comes to God in Christ, has God got your voice? And can you talk to your schoolmates about the Lord Jesus? Can you say a word about Him? Do you dare do it? Do you dare bow your head in a half minute silence before you eat? Does your voice belong to God?

And then I notice that their voices were both modest and reverent. For they covered their feet and they covered their faces. And I suppose the only reason for the covering of their faces was the presence of the Holy God. They reverently covered their faces. Reverence is a beautiful thing, and it's so rare in this terrible day and age in which we live. Some churches try to superinduce reverence by putting up statues and having windows with the light filtering through and having carpet on the floor, but they don't succeed. They only make you feel peculiar, and, you know, we all feel like it's a funeral. But a man who has passed the veil and looked even briefly upon the holy face of Isaiah's God can never be irreverent again. There will be a reverence in his spirit! And instead of boasting, he will cover his feet modestly.

I wish the ninety-nine and nine-tenths percent of all these world travelers, religious and non-religious, would cover their feet when they come home from far places. I am fed up to the chin with these wonder boys who just go places and then come home and entertain you for an offering and tell you where they've been. O brother, put a jackass in a boxcar in St. Louis and send him to Omaha, and when he gets there he's still a jackass. Put him in the boxcar and send him back, and when he gets back he's still a jackass. And yet we have the mistaken notion that if a fellow gets in a machine and flies around the world and comes back he's been transformed! No, he hasn't been transformed. He's just gotten more geography under his feet. Any ordinary duck can do that. A duck starts in Canada and flies to Florida and he's put geography under his feet. The next spring he comes back again.

Men are making money and they've got big socks full of green bills that they got from gullible church people. They wanted to tell you about where they've been. I don't know and I don't care where they've been. I want to know where they're going. That's all that matters. Where are you going, brother?

I have a lot of sympathy for the red cap in one of these hotels—these bell boys. A fellow came in and he had his suitcase just plastered from all of those airlines. He flew all around the world. And this bell boy thought, *Perhaps he'll tip me if I clean the thing.* So he got an eraser and he took it all off. And when the fellow came back, here was his suitcase clean as a pin. He'd taken all the labels off. He had ruined the fellow's reputation, you know. And now when he walked around nobody knows where he's been! But I don't care where he's been anyhow, because a dumbbell can go to Germany and come back a dumbbell still!

Abraham Lincoln never got out of the States, and Jesus never got out of Palestine. For years, they tried to send me everywhere and pay my way, and I could have gone and even have had a soda extra thrown in. When God tells me to go, I'll go. But I wouldn't go just for the going. Particularly, I wouldn't come back and spend other people's time telling them about it.

They covered their feet. They must have been somewhere, because they had feet and wings. They must certainly have been somewhere, but they hid their feet so people wouldn't know where they'd been. They could've said, "Look where I've been! Look what I have seen!" . . .

And then they reverently covered their faces before God Almighty, because here was the great God. Their worship was pure and spontaneous, it was voluntary and it was fervent. The word *seraphim* means "a fiery burner." I'm wondering how about you? How much fire have you got inside you? These creatures, these wondrous creatures inhabiting that other world, worship God day and night in His temple. They were called burners.

How fervent you are? Jesus said to the church, "Thou has left thy first love" (Rev. 2:4). That means first in degree of love, not first in time. You don't love me with the fervency with which you used to love me, He says. This grieves God and indicates backsliding in the heart of the individual. These burners are before us as examples. And we're called by God to look heavenward and see, they've served Him there day and night with fervency of spirit. How about my heart?

Brother, I want to ask you: Are you a fervent Christian? Are you warmhearted to the point of heat? Is there fire inside your spirit? You're religious, all right, and you know you're converted. But are you filled with fire? "He shall baptize you with the Holy Ghost and with fire" (Matt. 3:11). Some have tried to say that means judgment all around, but when the Holy Ghost came, He came as fire, so that ought to settle that.

It's fire we need, inward fervency that glows, that boils. Talk about diathermy. Somebody used the term in my hearing today.

Diathermy, meaning heating clear through! I believe in spiritual diathermy. I believe that God wants to heat the spirit clear, all the way through. And suddenly we're awakened to the fact that heaven and earth are full of the glory of the Lord.

An old Englishman said, "You never enjoy the world aright"—that is, the sinful world, not God's natural world—"Your enjoyment of the world is never right, till every morning you awake in heaven; see yourself in your Father's Palace; and look upon the skies, the earth, and the air as Celestial Joys: having such a reverend esteem of all, as if you were among the Angels. The bride of a monarch, in her husband's chamber, hath too such causes of delight as you." This quote can be found in: Traherne, Thomas. "Centuries of Meditations." London. 1908.

Brethren, we ought not to be satisfied by being merely Christians. We've ridden that term until it's almost offensive to hear it. "I'm born again. I'm born again," you say. Well, I know. You're born again. Thank God, or else you'd never see the kingdom. It's the business of a day-old baby to get busy and grow, develop, do something in the world before he falls asleep. And the business of a born-again Christian is to enter into the fullness of the Holy Ghost—to surrender his hands and feet and wings and voice and brains and presence and all to Jesus Christ and to be filled with the fire of His love.

Friends, our trouble is the absence of ecstasy. The seraphim were ecstatic. And we claim to be followers of the Lamb and worshipers of the King, but we're lukewarm and cold, and our notes are flat and without vibrancy. May God do something for us.

WORSHIP EVERY DAY OF THE WEEK

I will extol the LORD at all times;
his praise will always be on my lips.

PSALM 34:1

D o you quietly bow your head in reverence when you step into the average gospel church?

I am not surprised if your answer is no.

There is grief in my spirit when I go into the average church, for we have become a generation rapidly losing all sense of divine sacredness in our worship. Many whom we have raised in our churches no longer think in terms of reverence—which seems to indicate they doubt that God's presence is there.

In too many of our churches, you can detect the attitude that anything goes. It is my assessment that losing the awareness of God in our midst is a loss too terrible ever to be appraised.

Much of the blame must be placed on the growing acceptance of a worldly secularism that seems much more appealing in our church circles than any hungering or thirsting for the spiritual life that pleases God. We secularize God, we secularize the gospel of Christ and we secularize worship.

No great and spiritually powerful man of God is going to come out of such a church. No great spiritual movement of believing prayer and revival is going to come out of such a church. If God is to be honored and revered and truly worshiped, He may have to sweep us away and start somewhere else.

There is a necessity for true worship among us. If God is who He says He is, and if we are the believing people of God we claim to be, we must worship Him. I do not believe that we will ever truly delight in the adoring worship of God if we have never met Him in personal, spiritual experience through the new birth from above, wrought by the Holy Spirit of God Himself!

We have such smooth, almost secularized ways of talking people into the kingdom of God that we can no longer find men and women willing to seek God through the crisis of encounter. When we bring them into our churches, they have no idea of what it means to love and worship God because, in the route through which we have brought them, there has been no personal encounter, no personal crisis, no need of repentance—only a Bible verse with a promise of forgiveness.

Oh, how I wish I could adequately set forth the glory of that One who is worthy to be the object of our worship! I do believe that if our new converts—the babes in Christ—could be made to see His thousand attributes and even partially comprehend His being, they would become faint with a yearning desire to worship and honor and acknowledge Him, now and forever.

I know that many discouraged Christians do not truly believe in God's sovereignty. In that case, we are not filling our role as the humble and trusting followers of God and His Christ.

And yet, that is why Christ Jesus came into our world. The old theologians called it theanthropism—the union of the divine and human natures in Christ. This is a great mystery, and I stand in awe before it. I take off my shoes and kneel before this burning bush, this mystery I do not understand.

The theanthropy is the mystery of God and man united in one person—not two persons, but two natures.

So, the nature of God and the nature of man are united in this One who is our Lord Jesus Christ. All that is God and all that is man are in Christ fused eternally and inextricably.

Consider the experience of Moses in the desert as he beheld the fire that burned in the bush without consuming it. Moses had no hesitation in kneeling before the bush and worshiping God. Moses was not worshiping a bush; it was God and His glory dwelling in the bush that Moses worshiped.

That is an imperfect illustration, for when the fire departed from that bush it was a bush again.

But this Man, Christ Jesus, is eternally the Son. In the fullness of this mystery there has never been any departure, except for that awful moment when Jesus cried, "My God, my God, why hast thou forsaken me?" (Matt. 27:46). The Father turned His back for a moment when the Son took on Himself that putrefying mass of our sin and guilt, dying on the cross not for His own sin, but for ours.

The deity and the humanity never parted. And to this day, they remain united in that one Man. When we kneel before

Him and say, "Thy throne, O God, is for ever and ever" (Ps. 45:6), we are talking to God.

I think the prophets of God saw farther into the centuries and into the mysteries of God than we can with our great modern telescopes and electronic means of measuring light-years and planets and galaxies.

The prophets saw the Lord our God. They saw Him in His beauty, and they tried to describe Him.

They described Him as radiantly beautiful and fair, a winsome being. They said that He was royal and that He was gracious. They described Him as a majestic being; and yet they noted His meekness. They saw Him as righteous and filled with truth. They tried to describe the manner of His love, with its gladness and joy and fragrance.

When the prophets try to describe for me the attributes, the graces, the worthiness of the God who appeared to them and dealt with them, I feel that I can kneel down and follow their admonition: "He is thy Lord—worship thou Him."

He is fair and He is kingly, yet He is gracious in a sense that takes nothing away from His majesty.

He is meek, but it is the kind of meekness that likewise takes nothing away from His majesty.

The meekness and the majesty of Jesus. I wish I could write a hymn about that or compose music about it. Where else can you find majesty and meekness united?

The meekness was His humanity. The majesty was His deity. You find them everlastingly united in Him. So meek that he nursed at His mother's breast, cried like any baby, and needed all the human care that every child needs.

But He was also God, and in His majesty, He stood before Herod and before Pilate. When He returns, coming down from the sky, it will be in His majesty, the majesty of God. Yet it will also be in the majesty of the Man who is God.

This is our Lord Jesus Christ. Before His foes, He stands in majesty. Before His friends, He comes in meekness.

It is given to men and women to choose—a person may have either side. If he does not want the meek side of Jesus, he will come to know the majestic side.

On earth, the children came to Him. The sick and the sinful came to Him. The devil-possessed man came to Him. Those who knew their needs came from everywhere and touched Him, finding Him so meek that His power went out to them and healed them.

When He appears to men again, it will be in majesty. In His kingly majesty, He will deal with the pride and conceit and self-sufficiency of mankind, for the Bible says that every knee will bow and every tongue will confess that He is Lord and King.

To really know Him is to love and worship Him.

As God's people, we are so often confused that we could be known as God's poor, stumbling, bumbling people. That must be true of a great number of us, for we always think of worship as something we do when we go to church.

We call it God's house. We have dedicated it to Him. So we continue with the confused idea that it must be the only place where we can worship Him.

We come to the Lord's house, made out of brick and wood and lined with carpeting. We are used to hearing a call to worship:

"The Lord is in his holy temple; let all the earth keep silence before him" (Hab. 2:20).

That is on Sunday, and that is in church. Very nice!

But Monday morning comes soon. The Christian layman goes to his office. The Christian school teacher goes to the classroom. The Christian mother is busy with duties in the home.

On Monday, as we go about our different duties and tasks, are we aware of the presence of God? The Lord desires still to be in His holy temple, wherever we are. He wants the continuing love and delight and worship of His children, wherever we work.

Is it not a beautiful thing for a businessman to enter his office on Monday morning with an inner call to worship: "The Lord is in my office—let all the world be silent before Him."

If you cannot worship the Lord in the midst of your responsibilities on Monday, it is not very likely that you were worshiping on Sunday!

Actually, none of us has the ability to fool God. Therefore, if we are so engaged in our Saturday pursuits that we are far from His presence and far from a sense of worship on Saturday, we are not in very good shape to worship Him on Sunday.

I guess many people have an idea that they have God in a box. He is just in the church sanctuary, and when we leave and drive toward home, we have a rather faint, homesick feeling that we are leaving God in the big box.

You know that is not true, but what are you doing about it?

God is not confined to a building any more than He is confined to your car or your home or the office where you work.

Paul's earnest exhortation to the Corinthian Christians is just as valid for our lives today as it was when he expressed it: "Know ye not that ye are the temple of God, and that the Spirit of God dwelleth in you? If any man defile the temple of God, him shall God destroy; for the temple of God is holy, which temple ye are" (1 Cor. 3:16–17).

If you do not know the presence of God in your office, your factory, your home, then God is not in the church when you attend.

I became a Christian when I was a young man working in one of the tire factories in Akron, Ohio. I remember my work there. I remember my worship there, too. I had plenty of worshipful tears in my eyes. No one ever asked me about them, but I would not have hesitated to explain them.

You can learn to use certain skills until they are automatic. I became so skillful that I could do my work, and then I could worship God even while my hands were busy.

I have come to believe that when we are worshiping—and it could be right at the drill in the factory—if the love of God is in us and the Spirit of God is breathing praise within us, all the musical instruments in heaven are suddenly playing in full support.

Well, it is my experience that our total lives, our entire attitude as persons, must be toward the worship of God.

What is there in you that strives to worship God? Faith, love, obedience, loyalty, conduct of life—all of these strive in you to worship God. If there is anything within you that refuses to worship, there is nothing within you, then, that worships God very well.

You are not worshiping God as you should if you have departmentalized your life so that some areas worship and other parts do not worship.

This can be a great delusion—that worship only happens in church or in the midst of a dangerous storm or in the presence of some unusual and sublime beauty of nature around us. I have been with some fellows who became very spiritual when they stood on the breathtaking curve of a steep mountain cliff!

Occasionally we are in some situation like that and a person begins to yell, "Hooray for Jesus!"—or some other corny expression.

My brother or sister, if we are believing children of God in whom the Holy Spirit nurtures continual joy, delight and wonder, we will not need a storm on the mountain to show us how glorious our Lord really is.

It is a delusion to think that because we suddenly feel expansive and poetic in the presence of the storm or stars or space that we are spiritual. I need only remind you that drunkards or tyrants or criminals can have those "sublime" feelings, too. Let us not imagine that they constitute worship.

I can offer no worship wholly pleasing to God if I know that I am harboring elements in my life that are displeasing to Him. I cannot truly and joyfully worship God on Sunday and not worship Him on Monday. I cannot worship God with a glad song on Sunday and then knowingly displease Him in my business dealings on Monday and Tuesday.

I repeat my view of worship—*no worship is wholly pleasing to God until there is nothing in me displeasing to God.*

Is that a view that seems very discouraging to you?

Let me say that if you listen to me long enough you will receive some encouragement in the Spirit, but I have never had an inclination within me to encourage people in the flesh.

I have never had very much faith in people—as people. I do respect the good intentions that people have. I know they mean well. But in the flesh they cannot fulfill their good intentions. That is because we are sinners and we are all in a predicament—until we find the source of victory and joy and blessing in Jesus Christ.

There is nothing in either of us that can be made good until Jesus Christ comes and changes us—until He lives in us and unites our nature with God, the Father Almighty. Not until then can we call ourselves good.

That is why I say that your worship must be total. It must involve the whole you. That is why you must prepare to worship God, and that preparation is not always pleasant. There may be revolutionary changes which must take place in your life.

If there is to be true and blessed worship, some things in your life must be destroyed, eliminated. The gospel of Jesus Christ is certainly positive and constructive. But it must be destructive in some areas, dealing with and destroying certain elements that cannot remain in a life pleasing to God.

There have always been professing Christians who argue: "I worship in the name of Jesus." They seem to believe that worship of God is a formula. They seem to think there is a kind of magic in saying the name of Jesus.

Study the Bible carefully with the help of the Holy Spirit and you will find that the name and the nature of Jesus are one. It is not enough to know how to spell Jesus' name. If we have come to be like Him in nature, if we have come to the place of being able to ask in accordance with His will, He will give us the good things we desire and need. We do not worship in name only. We worship God as the result of a birth from above in which God has been pleased to give us more than a name. He has given us a nature transformed.

Peter expressed that truth this way: "Whereby are given unto us exceeding great and precious promises: that by these ye might be partakers of the divine nature, having escaped the corruption that is in the world through lust" (2 Peter 1:4).

Why should we delude ourselves about pleasing God in worship? If I live like a worldly and carnal tramp all day and then find myself in a time of crisis at midnight, how do I pray to a God who is holy? How do I address the One who has asked me to worship Him in spirit and in truth? Do I get on my knees and call on the name of Jesus because I believe there is some magic in that name?

If I am still the same worldly, carnal tramp, I will be disappointed and disillusioned. If I am not living in the true meaning of His name and His nature, I cannot properly pray in that name. If I am not living in His nature, I cannot rightly pray in that nature.

How can we hope to worship God acceptably when these evil elements remain in our natures undisciplined, uncorrected, unpurged, unpurified? Even granted that a man with evil ingredients in his nature might manage through some part of himself to worship God half-acceptably. But what kind of a way is that in which to live and continue?

"I want to dwell in your thoughts," God has been saying. "Make your thoughts a sanctuary in which I can dwell."

I do not have to do something wrong to feel blistering conviction and repent. I can lose fellowship with God, lose the keen sense of His presence, and lose the blessing of spiritual victory by thinking wrong.

I have found that God will not dwell in spiteful and polluted thoughts. He will not dwell in lustful and covetous thoughts. He will not dwell in proud and selfish thoughts.

God tells us to make a sanctuary of our thoughts in which He can dwell. He treasures our pure and loving thoughts, our meek and charitable and kindly thoughts. These are the thoughts like His own.

As God dwells in your thoughts, you will be worshiping, and God will be accepting. He will be smelling the incense of your high intention even when the cares of life are intense and activity is all around you.

If God knows that your intention is to worship Him with every part of your being, He has promised to cooperate with you. On His side is the love and grace, the promises and the atonement, the constant help and the presence of the Holy Spirit.

On your side there is determination, seeking, yielding, believing. Your heart becomes a chamber, a sanctuary, a shrine in which there may be continuous, unbroken fellowship and communion with God. Your worship rises to God moment by moment.

Two of Spurgeon's greatest sermons were "God in The Silence" and "God in The Storm." The heart that knows God can find God anywhere. I surely join with Spurgeon in the truth that a person filled with the Spirit of God, a person who has met God in a living encounter, can know the joy of worshiping Him, whether in the silences of life or in the storms of life.

There really is no argument. We know what God wants us to be. He wants us to be worshipers!

WORSHIP OUR BELOVED

Many waters cannot quench love; rivers cannot sweep it away. If one were to give all the wealth of one's house for love, it would be utterly scorned.

SONG OF SONGS 8:7

Now our Lord Jesus Christ is the shepherd. This has been believed by the church from the beginning. And the redeemed church is the fair bride. And in an hour of distress she tells the daughters of Jerusalem, "If ye find my beloved, that ye tell him, that I am sick of love" (Song 5:8). And of course they essentially ask her the question, "Why do you come to us like this? We have boyfriends too. We know lots of fine young men. What is it about your beloved? More than any other beloved you'd send us over the country telling, hunting him up to tell him the bride is sick of love."

She answered them, "His mouth is most sweet: yea, he is

altogether lovely. This is my beloved, and this is my friend, O daughters of Jerusalem" (v. 16).

And to the question "What is thy beloved more than another beloved?" David answers in the forty-fifth Psalm: "Thou art fairer than the children of men: grace is poured into thy lips: therefore God hath blessed thee for ever. Gird thy sword upon thy thigh, O most mighty, with thy glory and thy majesty. And in thy majesty ride prosperously because of truth and meekness and righteousness" (vv. 2–4). He goes on to describe Him in what he calls a "good matter" (v. 1)—touching the king. His pen is the pen of a ready writer. His tongue is the pen of a ready writer.

Peter rises higher than all of them put together and simply says in one great broad sweep, "He is Lord of all" (Acts 10:36).

Now this is our beloved. This is the one we have been born to worship. This is the one whom God made us to worship. And let's consider what He is the Lord of.

He is Lord of wisdom, and in Him is hidden all wisdom and all knowledge. And they are hidden away. And all the deep eternal purposes are His. Because of His perfect wisdom, He is enabled to play the checkers across the board of the universe and across the board of time and eternity, making everything work out right.

I don't mind saying to you, dear people, that if all I knew of Christianity was what I'm hearing these days, I don't think I'd be too interested. I don't think I'd be much interested in the Christ who was always trying to get something out of me. Always something. You don't have it, and He had it, and go to Him and now you have it—well, that's all part of the Bible of course, but it's rather the lower side of it. The higher side of it is who He is and whom we're called to worship.

What is thy beloved?

Not a word was said there about what he had for her. Just the fact that he was something. She described him in language that could be indelicate in her passionate outpouring. What is your beloved? "Why," she said, "he's right and ready and he's chiefest among ten thousand, and his eyes are like the eyes of doves by the rivers of water washed with milk. And his cheeks are a bed of spices, and his lips are like lilies dropping sweet smelling myrrh. His mouth is sweet. Yea, he is altogether lovely."

And she didn't say, "Why? Don't you know why I love him? Because when I'm tired, he rests me. And when I'm afraid, he takes my fear away. And when I want a job, he gets it for me. And when I want a bigger car, I ask him. When I want to have health, he heals me." No, He helps His people, and I believe! A young man prayed a year for a car, and God did that for him. I believe in that. I believe that God does those things for people.

In the first few years of my ministry, if I couldn't pray for those things, I would have starved to death. And not only that, I would have brought my wife down with me. So I believe in answered prayer, all right. But that's not all. That's the lowest section of the Bible.

He is the Lord of all wisdom. And He is the Lord, the Father of the everlasting ages. Not the "everlasting Father" (Isa. 9:6) as it says in our King James Version, but the Father of the everlasting ages. He lays out the ages like an architect lays out his blueprint. He lays out the ages like a real estate development man lays out a small town and then builds. He lays it out and then builds hundreds of houses on it. So He is not dealing with buildings and local developments; He's dealing with the agents. And He is the Lord of all wisdom, and because He's perfect in wisdom, He is able to do all this. And history is the slow development of His purposes, you see.

You take on a house that is being built. The architect has drawn it down to the last tiny little dot and tiny little x. He knows everything about it and he's written his name right there on the bottom of the blueprint and turned it over to the contractor, and he has farmed it out to the electrician, and the plumber, and all the rest. And you go down there sometime and you say casually, "I wonder what that's going to be? It's a mess now. There it is. They're steam shoveling there with this great ugly nose plowing out a hole and throwing the dirt up on the bank or in trucks to haul away. And they're unloading bricks there. It's just a confused conglomeration of this and that."

You say, "What's this?" and then you return six or eight to ten months later, and you see a charming house. The landscapers have even been there, and the trees, the evergreens, are standing there with little green spikes beside the windows, and it's a beautiful thing. And there is a child playing on the lawn.

Well, we ask you to believe, my friends, that the Father of the everlasting ages, the Lord of all wisdom, has laid out His plans, and He's working toward them. And you and I go by, and we see a church all mixed up, and we see her sore, distressed by schisms, rent asunder by heresy. We see her back-slidden in one part of the world, we see her confused in another part of the world, and we shrug our shoulders and say, "What is thy beloved, anyway? What is all this?"

And the answer is: He is the Lord of the wise ages and He's laying it all out. What you're seeing now is only the steam shovel working. That's all. Only the truck backed up with bricks. That's what you're seeing. You're only seeing workmen in overalls going about, killing time. That's all you're seeing. You're just seeing people, and people make you sick because of the way we do. The way we backslide and tumble around and get mixed up and run after willow wisps and think it's the Shekinah glory, and hear an owl hoot and think it's the silver trumpet and take off in the wrong directions, spend the century catching up on ourselves and backing up, and history smiles at us.

But don't be too sure, brother. Come back in another millennium or so, and see what the Lord of all wisdom has done with what He's got. See then what He's done. He's the Lord of all wisdom, and history is the slow development of His purposes.

He's the Lord of all righteousness. You know what? I'm glad that I'm attached to something good—that there's something good somewhere in the universe. Now, I couldn't possibly be a Pollyanna. I was born wrong. I had to have a different father and mother and a different ancestral line back at least ten generations for me to have been a Napoleon—a plumb pudding philosopher who believed that everything was good, and I can't believe that. I don't think it's true. There's so much that isn't right everywhere, and we might as well admit it. If you don't believe it, leave your car unlocked.

And then we've got the Pharisees who think they're righteous, and they're not. They're just self-righteous hypocrites. And we've got politicians that lie and make all kinds of promises which they don't intend to keep, and the only honest one that I've known of in my lifetime has been Wendell Willkie. When somebody challenged him with promises that he made during a campaign he said, "Those were just campaign promises." He was the only one that I know who was honest enough to admit he lied to get elected. He didn't get elected, but he lied anyhow and he admitted it, which was something.

Righteousness is not found. If you think it is, get on a bus somewhere when there's a crowd, and you'll find that no matter how old and feeble you are, you'll get a rib or two cracked or at least badly dinged by the elbow of some housewife on her way home. Bless you. We're just not good. People are just not good.

Among the first things we learn to do, we learn something bad and something mean. Sin is everywhere. I want to be joined to something good. You say, "Well, I'm an American." I'm an American, too. I was born here, and it didn't cost me a dime to become an American. It cost my father a little and my mother, but it didn't cost me a dime. I'm an American and I'll never be anything else. And when they bury me, there will be a little bit of America, as the poet said, "wherever I may be placed." But you've got to be an awful sissy to believe in the total righteousness of the United States of America. Don't you? You've got to be an awful fool. That buzzard's nest up there in Washington—God bless them—it doesn't make any difference whether they're Democrats or Republicans. A bunch of them are crooks and they mean alright, but they're Adam's fallen brood and they're doing the best they can. We'd probably do worse. We can just pray for them and ask God to have mercy on them. But that's about it.

You try to turn on the radio to get something educational or something cultural, and all you get is songs sung about automobiles and cigarettes. Well, it's not a good world we live in. It's a bad world. And you can become a Protestant, but that doesn't help much. And you can become an American or be an American, but that doesn't help too much, either. But when you attach yourself to the Lord of glory, you're connected with something that really is righteous. Not Pollyanna-ish, but something really righteous. He is righteousness itself. The call of the concept of righteousness and all of the possibility of righteousness are all summed up in Him.

But under the sun, David says,

> Thy throne, O God, is for ever and ever: the sceptre of thy kingdom is a right sceptre.
>
> Thou lovest righteousness, and hatest wickedness: therefore God, thy God, hath anointed thee with the oil of gladness above thy fellows. (Ps. 45:6–7)

So we have there a perfectly righteous Savior. They spied on Him; they sent the enemy to search into His life. Can you imagine if Jesus' foot had slipped once, even once down the line? Can you imagine if Jesus had lost His temper once? Or if Jesus had been selfish once? Can you imagine if Jesus had done one thing that you and I take for granted even once? Can you imagine that all the sharp, beady eyes of hell were following Him trying to catch something out of His mouth? And when the end of His days had almost come, He turned on them and said, "Which of you convinceth me of sin? And if I say the truth, why do ye not believe me?" (John 8:46).

Righteousness was His, and He's the High Priest. And if you go back to the Old Testament, you'll find that when the high priest went into the holy place, he wore on his shoulder and on his breast certain things that were prescribed, and on his forehead he wore a miter. And who knows what was on that miter? Holiness unto the Lord. He was saying the best he could. Even that man had to have a sacrifice made for himself. But He was trying to say in symbol what's been fulfilled in fact, that when He, the High Priest of all high priests came, He would wear on His forehead holiness unto the Lord. And when they, in mockery, crashed down that crown of thorns upon His brow, if they'd had the eyes of a prophet, they could've seen a miter there. Holiness unto the Lord. He is the Lord of all righteousness.

He is the Lord of all mercy because He establishes His kingdom of reclaimed rebels. He redeemed them and He won them and He renews the right spirit within them. Everybody in His kingdom is a redeemed rebel.

You know what we think about people that have betrayed our country? We scarcely forgive them. We may forgive them, but we always look askance at them. Those who have fallen as some have into Communism and have spied, or at least helped the Communist scheme, and have gotten their eyes open and turned away from it, gone to the FBI and admitted it, gone and straightened their lives out—even them we look at with a bit of doubt. But did you ever stop to think that Jesus Christ hasn't got a single member of His kingdom that wasn't a former spy and rebel for the enemy? It's bad for a man in Washington or Oak Hill or the

University of Chicago to get secrets and take them and tell them to the enemy. It's bad, and they hang them for it. How much worse to be over on the side of the enemy against the Lord of glory as all sinners are. And don't forget it: all sinners are.

That's why I smile when I see an old, self-satisfied deacon, sitting with his hands crossed looking like a statue of St. Francis. He is a very godly man, indeed, and very conscious of it. "All right, Deacon Jones, don't you know what you were? You were a rebel and a spy! And you sold out the secrets of the kingdom of God and collaborated with the enemy and lived to overthrow it." That's all of us, and there isn't a one of us that doesn't include. If you don't like that, then you're no theologian. And if you knew your Bible, you'd agree with me, because that's what we all were. But mercy, O the mercy, Lord of all mercy!

Sometime I want to preach a sermon on mercy. I don't think I ever have. I, of course, have woven it into all of my preaching, but think of the mercy of the Lord Jesus Christ. He is the Lord of all righteousness, and we are bad, but He is also the Lord of all mercy. So in His great kindness, He takes rebels and unrighteous persons, sinners, and makes them His own. He establishes them in righteousness and renews a right spirit within them. Then we have a church. We have a cell—a company of believers—together, and He is their Lord.

He is the Lord of all power. Consider this Scripture:

And after these things I heard a great voice of much people in heaven, saying, Alleluia; Salvation, and glory, and honour, and power, unto the Lord our God: for true and righteous are his judgments: for he hath judged the great whore, which did corrupt the earth with her fornication, and hath avenged the blood of his servants at her hand. And again they said, Alleluia. And her smoke rose up for ever and ever. And the four and twenty elders and the four beasts fell down and worshipped God that sat on the throne, saying, Amen; Alleluia. (Rev. 19:1–4)

Here we have no hysteria but a lot of ecstasy. "And a voice came out of the throne, saying, Praise our God, all ye his servants, and ye that fear him, both small and great" (v. 5).

And then, [I imagine] John said, "It'd be worth getting put in a salt mine on the island of Patmos to have a vision like that, wouldn't it?" It really would. They say they had him in a salt mine over there on the island of Patmos. That fellow who lived out on the sea catching fish, and walked the sandy shores, and smelled the fresh air—now he's in a mine. It's dark in there, and suddenly the Lord lifts him into the spirit on the Lord's day, and he hears a voice saying, "Let us be glad and rejoice, and give honour to him: for the marriage of the Lamb is come, and his wife hath made herself ready" (v. 7).

See, there's the Song of Solomon in the New Testament:

And to her was granted that she should be arrayed in fine linen, clean and white: for the fine linen is the righteousness of saints.

And he saith unto me, Write, Blessed are they which are called unto the marriage supper of the Lamb. And he saith unto me, These are the true sayings of God. And I fell at his feet to worship him. And he said unto me, See thou

do it not: I am thy fellowservant, and of thy brethren that
have the testimony of Jesus: worship God: for the testimony of Jesus is the spirit of prophecy.

And I saw heaven opened. (vv. 8–11)

"I saw heaven open," as Moses did and Isaiah did and Ezekiel
did and John did, and I'm waiting around.

And behold a white horse; and he that sat upon him was
called Faithful and True, and in righteousness he doth
judge and make war. His eyes were as a flame of fire, and
on his head were many crowns; and he had a name written,
that no man knew, but he himself. And he was clothed
with a vesture dipped in blood: and his name is called The
Word of God. (vv. 11–13)

There we have this victorious Lord Jesus Christ, the Lord of all
power. You know, sin has scarred the world.

Back in the state of Pennsylvania, they do what they call "strip
mining," and I was angry in my heart when I saw what they'd
done to our lovely Pennsylvania hills. These greedy dogs had gone
and with their great machinery, stripped away the foliage, gone
down into the bowels of the beautiful hillsides, and taken out a
cheap coal. Anything to get a little money. And the government
says, "When you take it in strip mine, you've gotta fill it up again,
or it'll cost you $100 per acre." And they grin and say, "It'll cost
us more than $100 an acre to fill it up," so they pay their fine and
leave it there!

When I was back there this last summer and drove up past the old place. When I was there four or five years before, it lay there like a wounded man, all gouged and ugly. In my boyhood days, it had been beautiful to see, as the green trees met the blue sky above. But then it was scarred. And they paid their fine because it was cheaper than to fulfill their promise. They left her there, that lovely hillside, all gouged and cut and bruised. But when I was back last summer, I could've wept to see how kindly Mother Nature had gone to work. Where four or five years before it was just an ugly hole, now the sun and the rain and the wind and the waves I've seen fall many times on that hillside had begun to bring out the blossoms that I didn't know were there. And now Nature is covering up her wounds, her scars, her ugliness.

God made the world beautiful, and if you go out and make it ugly, God, in five years, will make it beautiful again. The human race is ugly, though made in the image of God. Potentialities of beauty, ugly in its sin. I think, my brethren, that the ugliest place in the universe is hell. And when a man says, "Ugly as hell," he's using a proper and valid comparison, for there is nothing more ugly than hell. Surely hell is the ugliest place in the universe. It is that against which all other ugliness can be compared, and surely heaven is the most beautiful place, the place of supreme beauty. . . . The peace of all the faithful and the calm of all the blessed in violet and very divineness shall all be there. So as hell is the ugliest place in the universe, surely the most beautiful place will be heaven, for all harmony will be there and all fragrance and all its charm.

But between heaven, which is the epitome of all supreme beauty, and hell, which is the essence of all ugliness, there lies the poor, scarred world. Poor earth lies like a pitiful dying woman, clothed in rags that once was a beauty that could have stood and been admired by the ages. Now sin has cut her down, and she's tattered and torn. From the Nile to the Mississippi, from California to Bangkok, from the North Pole to the South Pole—wherever human beings go, we find more ugliness and sin and hatred and suspicion and name-calling and all the rest. And the beautiful race that the Lord made to be His bride now in her pathetic ugliness lies dying, clothed in rags. But Jesus Christ, the Lord of mercy, came to save her, and took upon Himself her flesh and was made in the likeness of man and for sin He gave Himself to die. And there's going to be a restoration.

Years ago I read that great book. I suppose it's one of the greatest books ever written of its kind, the great book by Victor Hugo. In it is one of the most pathetic and tender passages that I think I've ever read in all literature. You'd have to go to the Bible to find things as deep and moving.

Here was a young man, one of the upper class, the nobles, and here was the woman that he was in love with. And here in the middle was a pale-faced, little urchin girl from the streets of Paris who with her poor rags and her pale, tubercular face, also loved the nobleman but didn't dare say so. He used her to carry notes back and forth. And this fellow never dreamed that this poor sallow-faced girl dressed in rags had lost her heart to him and his nobility. So he went to find her and see what he could do to help her, and found her lying on a bed of rags in a tenement house in the low section of Paris. This time, she can't get up to greet him or carry a note to his fiancée.

He says to her, "What can I do for you?" And she says, "Well, I'm dying and I'll be gone in a moment." He said, "What can I do? Tell me." And she said, "Will you do one thing for me before I close my eyes for the last time? When I'm dead would you kiss my forehead?"

I know it was only Victor Hugo's brilliant imagination, but I know Victor Hugo had seen that in Paris. He'd gone through the sewers there and he'd seen this. He knew about it, and he knew that you can beat a girl down and you can clothe her in rags and you can fill her with tuberculosis and you can make her so thin that the wind will blow her off course when she walks down a dirty street, but you can't take out her heart. That thing that makes her want to love a man—you can't take that out. God said to Adam, "You can't be alone. It's not right." And He made a woman for him. You can't take that out. Victor Hugo knew it, and he wrote that in.

I rarely quote from fiction, but I thought that was worth it. My dear friends, our Lord Jesus Christ came down and found the race like that—consumptive and long and pale-faced, dying. He took on Himself all her death and rose the third day, and took all the pathos out and all the pity out, and now she comes walking on the arm of her Beloved, walking into the presence of God. He presents her, not a poor, pitiful, recluse forehead he kissed when she was dead. But His happy, bright-eyed Bride, neat to be a partaker of the saints in Light. . . .

"He is thy Lord; and worship thou him" (Ps. 45:11).

REFERENCES

1: What Happened to Our Worship?

A. W. Tozer, *Whatever Happened to Worship: A Call to True Worship* (Chicago: Christian Publications, 1985; reprint and revised edition, WingSpread, 2012), 9–20.

2: Failing God

Whatever Happened to Worship, 85–95.

3: The Reason We Exist

A. W. Tozer, "A Definition of Worship" (sermon, Southside Alliance Church, Chicago, October 20, 1957).

4: True Worship Requires the New Birth

Whatever Happened to Worship, 21–32.

5: Worship as He Wills

A. W. Tozer, "He is Lord, Worship Him" (sermon, Southside Alliance Church, Chicago, September 22, 1957).

6: Worship He Who Is Majestic and Meek

A. W. Tozer, "Worship the Lord of Glory and Meekness" (sermon, Southside Alliance Church, Chicago, October 6, 1957).

7: Awed by God's Presence

Whatever Happened to Worship, 63–72.

8: Genuine Worship Involves Feeling

Whatever Happened to Worship, 73–83.

9: Worship Like the Seraphim

A. W. Tozer, "The Worship of the Seraphim and Our Worship" (sermon, Southside Alliance Church, Chicago, September 20, 1953).

10: Worship Every Day of the Week

Whatever Happened to Worship, 109–120.

11: Worship Our Beloved

A. W. Tozer, "A Look at our Worship of God" (sermon, Southside Alliance Church, Chicago, October 27, 1957).

THE TOZER ESSENTIALS

from MoodyPublishers.com

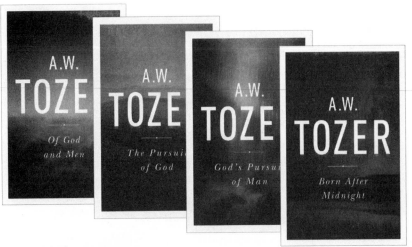

"When religion has said its last word, there is little that we
need other than God Himself."

—A.W. Tozer

Also available as eBooks

COMPLETE THE COLLECTION

from MoodyPublishers.com

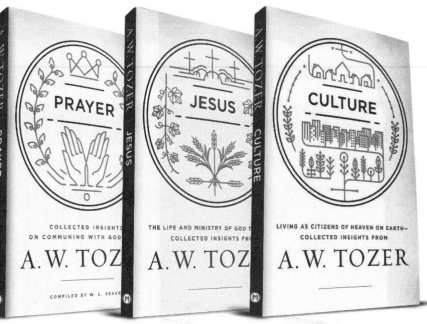

978-0-8024-1381-9   978-0-8024-1520-2   978-1-60066-801-2

"Tozer is one of the great Christian writers of this century. Reading him is like drinking at an oasis in the desert."

—Dr. J. I. Packer

Also available as eBooks

MOODY
Publishers®

From the Word to Life®

BOOKEND YOUR DAY WITH WISDOM

from MoodyPublishers.com

978-1-60066-794-7   978-1-60066-792-3

A.W. Tozer

Searching for more?

Visit **awtozer.org** to learn more about this
beloved spiritual author and browse
related resources.